"This is the best go-to book on how to use hope to relieve depression."

>—**Martin Seligman, PhD**, director of the Penn Positive
> Psychology Center, director of the master of applied
> positive psychology program at the University of
> Pennsylvania; and author of *Flourish*

"A life well lived is founded on meaning, purpose, and a higher calling. Moments of despair are opportunities for healing, and emotional and spiritual growth. Daniel Tomasulo's deep understanding of the entanglement of perceptions, experiences, emotions, and modes of thinking, envisioning, and actualizing worthy goals is the perfect recipe for fulfillment, joy, peace, and expansion of awareness."

>—**Deepak Chopra, MD**, author of *Metahuman*

"If you feel like you've lost your way, let Dan take your hand. He has in this beautiful book laid out the steps toward hope, and I cannot think of a wiser or more compassionate companion."

>—**Angela Duckworth**, founder and CEO of Character Lab,
> and *New York Times* bestselling author of *Grit*

"This is a must-read for therapists, as well as for anyone dealing with struggles and hardships (and that means all of us). The fact that this book has been written gives me hope!"

>—**Tal Ben Shahar**, *New York Times* bestselling author of
> *Even Happier*, *Happier*, and *Being Happy*

"Tomasulo has an unusual ability to simplify, and render vivid, complex ideas in ways that inspire trust."

—**George Vaillant, MD**, professor in the department
of psychiatry at Harvard Medical School,
former director of The Grant Study of Adult
Development, and author of *Triumphs of Experience*

"Dan Tomasulo is one of the most gifted writers, teachers, practitioners, and innovators in the field of positive psychology today. His new book on learned hopefulness is a thorough and well-researched guide to becoming more proactive, engaged, and purposeful in your life, regardless of where you start or where you hope to go. Part of Dan's noteworthy skill is that he seamlessly blends stories from his therapy world into cutting-edge research on flourishing, and then he offers analogies and unique exercises that make the reader take action. Putting down any one of Dan's books is hard because of their pull on your intellect and heart; this one is no different. Bravo!"

—**Caroline Adams Miller, MAPP**, international
bestselling author of *Getting Grit, Creating Your Best Life*,
and *My Name is Caroline*

"Chock-full of evidence-based exercises designed to alleviate depression and boost well-being, *Learned Hopefulness* is like having your own therapist. Read it with paper and pencil in hand."

—**Margaret H. Greenberg, MAPP, PCC**, executive coach,
and coauthor of *Profit from the Positive*

"Hope is one of our greatest superpowers; it can be discovered, rediscovered, uncovered, and built up—at the best of times and worst of times. Dan Tomasulo is a hope teacher. He embodies it and radiates it in his life. In this book, he shares it all. Whether you are high or low in the strength of hope, your well-being will soar by reading and practicing what awaits you in this important book."

—**Ryan M. Niemiec, PsyD**, psychologist; education
director of the renowned VIA Institute on Character;
and author or coauthor of eleven books, including
The Power of Character Strengths

"A warm and uplifting book about what is arguably our most important human capacity—hope. Drawing on his decades-long experience as a psychotherapist, as well as psychologist research, Tomasulo shows how each person can build more hope in their lives. In elegant prose, he makes a convincing case for how hope, in all its multifarious forms, helps people overcome depression and lead flourishing lives."

—**Emily Esfahani Smith**, author of *The Power of Meaning*

"'Happily ever after' may work in fairy tales. But in real life, *Learned Hopefulness* is the way to go for building healthy relationships!"

—**Suzie Pileggi Pawelski, MAPP, and
James O. Pawelski, Phd**, coauthors of *Happy Together*

"Finding hope, even in the darkest times, is the most important part of recovering from trauma.
Thank you, Dan, for the invaluable road map in *Learned Hopefulness*. With groundbreaking new research, simple—but hardly simplistic—analogies, and illustrations, we feel again what is possible."

—**Kim Scharnberg**, internationally renowned music arranger, composer, and producer of *From Broadway With Love*

"Tomasulo is a pioneer in applying positive psychology for deep transformation. His innovative methods taught to graduate students in our Spirituality Mind Body Institute at Teachers College, Columbia University, come alive in *Learned Hopefulness*. Using the very latest research findings to inform effective tools, this book is an open treasure chest for building personal fulfillment."

—**Lisa Miller, PhD**, professor and founder of the Spirituality Mind Body Institute, Teachers College, Columbia University; and *New York Times* bestselling author of *The Spiritual Child*

"You won't find a kinder, more thoughtful counseling psychologist than Dan Tomasulo. This book is the next best thing to a therapy session with him: it's grounded in science, filled with heartwarming stories, and brimming with hope."

—**Adam Grant**, *New York Times* bestselling author of *Give and Take* and *Originals*; and host of the chart-topping TED podcast, *WorkLife*

Learned Hopefulness

The Power of Positivity to Overcome Depression

Dan Tomasulo, PhD

New Harbinger Publications, Inc.

Publisher's Note

Distributed in Canada by Raincoast Books

Copyright © 2020 by Dan Tomasulo
New Harbinger Publications, Inc.
5674 Shattuck Avenue
Oakland, CA 94609
www.newharbinger.com

Cover design by Amy Shoup

Acquired by Jennye Garibaldi

Edited by Teja Watson

All Rights Reserved

Library of Congress Cataloging-in-Publication Data

Names: Tomasulo, Daniel J., author.
Title: Learned hopefulness / [by Dan Tomasulo]
Description: Oakland, CA : New Harbinger Publications, Inc., 2020. |
   Includes bibliographical references.
Identifiers: LCCN 2019058715 (print) | LCCN 2019058716 (ebook) | ISBN
   9781684034680 (paperback) | ISBN 9781684034697 (pdf) | ISBN
   9781684034703 (epub)
Subjects: LCSH: Positive psychology.
Classification: LCC BF204.6 .T66 2020 (print) | LCC BF204.6 (ebook) | DDC
   150.19/88--dc23
LC record available at https://lccn.loc.gov/2019058715
LC ebook record available at https://lccn.loc.gov/2019058716

Printed in the United States of America

22   21   20

10   9   8   7   6   5   4   3   2   1   First Printing

"Hope is the thing with feathers that perches in the soul and sings the tune without the words and never stops at all."

—*Emily Dickinson*

"A new baby is like the beginning of all things—wonder, hope, a dream of possibilities."

—*Eda LeShan*

This book is dedicated to my grandson,
Callahan Thomas Fetrow.

Contents

Foreword

In the late 1950s, the psychologist Ellis Paul Torrance brought an experiment to two elementary schools in Minneapolis to find the secret sauce of creative fulfillment. Nestled between a very large number of tests, he asked children a seemingly innocuous question: *What are you in love with?* He then followed up with the children during the next twenty years to see which of his tests could predict adult creativity.

Torrance was astonished that the extent to which children had a future image of themselves that they were in love with was a *better* predictor for creative fulfillment in adulthood than any of his tests for scholastic promise and school achievement. He wrote:

> "Life's most energizing and exciting moments occur in those split
> seconds when our struggling and searching are suddenly trans-
> formed into the dazzling aura of the profoundly new, an image of
> the future.... One of the most powerful wellsprings of creative
> energy, outstanding accomplishment, and self-fulfillment seems to
> be falling in love with something— your dream, your image of the
> future."[1]

Positive images of the future carry us forward to our destiny, despite the inevitable twists and turns of life. We each have a destiny, a best possible future. Yet we are constantly getting in our own way, losing sight of that future. In the process, we lose *hope*.

The humanistic psychologist Abraham Maslow argued that there are two very different realms of human existence. In the Deficiency Realm, we are motivated by what we lack. We try to force the world to conform, as if we are screaming "Love me!" "Accept me!" "Respect me!" Entering the Being Realm is like replacing a clouded lens with a clear lens. Suddenly we see the world and people for what they *actually* are—not as a means to our own end—but as an *end in themselves*. We admire the sacredness of each person and recognize they are on their own journey of self-actualization. We also open to opportunities for growth. When we are no longer primarily motivated by deficiency, we can explore the full richness of life—the joyful just as much as the forlorn—with curiosity and acceptance. Defenses down, we finally see the world's beauty clearly, as well as the beautiful possibilities in our lives.[2]

In recent years, psychologists have begun to chart the psychology behind imagination, hope, and possibility. What is becoming clear is that we don't need to be slaves to our past; we can navigate the future. There is a toolbox for hope, habits you can learn that will help you point a compass to your positive destiny. While much has been written about the toolbox of positive psychology, there has never existed a unifying theory of *hope*. Until now.

Dan Tomasulo has put together a gem of a resource, a once-in-a-lifetime reading experience. You will learn how to make a profound shift in perspective and set yourself free from the shackles of your mind. I can think of no better guide; Tomasulo is one of the most thoughtful, compassionate humans I know—not to mention an extraordinarily sensitive and insightful clinical positive psychologist.

This book is not Pollyannaish but *wise*. Tomasulo doesn't tell you to ignore the reality of your suffering; he teaches you how restore balance by increasing awareness and reframing what your future *could* be. This book will help you harness the gift of your imagination to get in touch—more deeply than you probably have ever been before—with your greatest strengths and highest possibilities in life.

In the framing of Maslow, this book will help you transcend the Deficiency Realm, and in the words of Tomasulo, tune into the "hope channel." You may have gone your entire life, up to this point, with a grainy picture of your future. While a clearer picture won't magically sweep all negative possibilities out of your life, you will learn to put them in perspective. By refocusing on the positive potential that already lies within, you will restore a greater sense of hope than you ever thought was possible.

Scott Barry Kaufman
November 28, 2019

Introduction

"Hope is not a form of guarantee; it's a form of energy, and very frequently that energy is strongest in circumstances that are very dark."

—*John Berger*

When my marriage capsized after thirty years of being together, I had to learn to be hopeful. Since you've picked up this book, perhaps something has arrived in your life without warning. Like a boat hitting an unseen iceberg, your ship sank, and you're fighting for your life. When these things happen, we may feel uncertain about how to move forward in our lives. I am not typically a depressed person. I am usually upbeat, have good energy, and take setbacks in stride. So as my wife and I separated and divorced, I was thrown for a loop by my somber mood, low energy, and the loss of my enthusiasm. Work was the hardest part. There's nothing worse than a depressed psychologist. I continued my clinical work, but it was difficult to listen to people talking about their depression when I could barely manage my own. *You think that's bad? Let me tell you what happened to me....*

Then I was introduced to positive psychology. My best friend was becoming a positive psychologist, and he encouraged me to try the techniques—for example, reviewing the previous day each morning through the lens of gratitude, or doing something kind for someone else. At first, this seemed like using a pea shooter to bring down a battleship. How could these small shifts manage the immense pain inside of me? But nothing else was helping. I needed help developing an appreciation for my life and my future again. Although it had never been a problem before, it now seemed impossible.

Everything I'd worked for, hoped for, and believed in seemed ruined. My vision of the future had become to simply survive it. Having gratitude and being kind to others was not my idea of getting better. It seemed too simple, too easy, not powerful enough to lift my low mood. I was dealing with financial, social, and emotional whiplash. How could reviewing my miserable day through the lens of gratitude change that?

My friend was persistent, though, and dragged me to the first International Positive Psychology Association conference, where I first learned of the profound and powerful research being done. If what they were proposing was even marginally true, psychology was on the brink of a new dawn. I learned that positive psychology is the study of strengths that empower people and communities to thrive, based on the belief that people want to live fulfilling and meaningful lives, and focused on how we can cultivate what is best within ourselves. The research is aimed at ways to feel more happy more often, by improving our experiences of love, work, and play. This mindset offered my first taste of genuine hope.

In its simplest form, the research awakened me to the possibility that it was feasible to change how I felt—to actually *transform* my feelings. Even with all my training, clinical work, and supervision, this was the first time I believed that dreary feelings could actually be altered, not just tolerated. This led me to embrace the findings of positive psychology, and the practices that taught me to hope again.

From Surviving to Thriving

The field of clinical psychology has traditionally focused on identifying the problems causing emotional pain and mental illness, and then working to alleviate symptoms. Do our methods—talk therapy of various kinds, sometimes medication—work? Yes. Do they work well, or in a way that lasts? In too many cases, no.[3] The fact is, 80 percent of people who recover from depression relapse.[4] If are reading this book, you may be one of them.

You may have found something that helped—therapy, medicine, diet changes, exercise, better sleep, more sunlight—but it may have worked only somewhat, or for some time. The effort succeeded, but it wasn't sustained. Why? Because traditional psychology and medicine were designed to do only half the job: they get us out of the hole, but they don't really keep us out. The cycle continues.

What about the 20 percent who recover and don't relapse? In a series of studies aimed at improving symptoms of depression, researchers found that simple methods focused on cultivating the best in themselves not only prevented participants from relapsing—they maintained sustainable levels of well-being for more than a year.[5] Not only did they learn how to steer clear of depression, but they also often learned to thrive.[6]

They learned *hopefulness*. As we'll see in these pages, hopefulness—or hope, as I'll also call it—is not so much a state of mind as it is a *habit* of mind, of heart. And habits can be changed. Hopefulness skills won't replace whatever treatments you've been using to control your depression. If you are taking medication, continue. If you have a physical routine that has been helpful, keep doing it. If you've developed healthy habits like exercise, good sleep, a nutritious diet—keep those up! They support your mental health as much as your physical health. If there are still changes you could make in these areas, what you learn in this book will help you lean into those changes.

Habits of heart, mind, and body affect our mood either positively or negatively. In this book, I will be emphasizing learned hopefulness as a collection of heart and mind habits designed to improve well-being. By focusing on the science of positive psychology, which highlights emotional well-being, we can maximize the impact that healthy strategies have on our lives. And you'll receive new tools to add to what you are already doing in your life.

Positive psychology practices will not only add to your toolbox to help you combat low moods, negative thoughts, and grief—but also shape and influence your positive attributes. Savoring, mindfulness, faith, hope, well-being, and optimism are just some of what you'll learn to cultivate. When you learn tools that both alleviate suffering *and* allow you to thrive, you learn how to get out of a bad place, stay out, and live a happier life.

The simple truth is this: not being depressed isn't the same as being happy. Whether you've struggled with milder or more severe forms of depression, you will learn ways to increase hope and be happier. The tools of traditional psychology focus on relieving distress. The tools of positive psychology promote well-being. The combination of the two leads to real and sustained change. These skills have the power to change how you experience the world.

Your Journey Through This Book

Not seeing the obstacles we put in our way, including our own decisions and thought cycles, is what keeps us stuck. Ruminating thoughts siphon our energy and block our positivity. The downward spiral of negative thinking is like a runaway train—leading us to perceive our situation as fixed and unchangeable. If you've ever felt too depleted to even try to get out of your depression—you are not alone.

We are drawn to the familiar, and if what's familiar is negative thinking, we'll have difficulty taking in the positive. It's a cycle, and this book will teach you how to break the cycle and get it spinning in the opposite direction—starting today. Some of the tools you'll learn in this book will help you untangle from the past, others will help you engage in the present, and more than a few will help you create your future. Some of the best practices can do all of this at once.

The book is organized the way I've learned to teach these principles. The first chapter will give you a working knowledge of positive psychology principles and the research behind their effectiveness in short-circuiting depressive spirals. It will also introduce you to some exercises, so you can begin to experience how effective these tools can be. Each of the next seven chapters teaches a choice you can make to learn hopefulness, and the tools to help develop these new habits. As they become habits, the tools get easier to access and use.

Decision Point	Tools for:
Seeing possibilities	Challenging beliefs about our limitations
Adjusting perception	Transforming negative beliefs into hopeful ones
Shaping feelings	Cultivating positive emotions
Exploring strengths	Discovering your best character qualities, to improve your life
Creating micro-goals	Setting goals calibrated to motivate you
Finding purpose	Developing life priorities and determining what matters
Cherishing relationships	Connecting to others and learning how to give and receive

Each of the seven chapters will introduce the main ideas we'll be working through, talk about the research, and teach you skills, tools, and practices through exploration exercises. All of this will build your hopefulness, resilience, and well-being. I will also use case studies as examples. All names and details have been masked, according to the American Psychological Association's guide for using case studies.

To keep track of your progress, I encourage you to keep a notebook—a journal that is either handwritten or digital. I'd like you to feel what happens when we do these explorations, so you can assess their effects. It will be most effective if you can do the exercises when you are prompted to. I know it's tempting to keep reading and do these tasks later, but doing them as we go will give you a real sense of what it's like to shift your perspective and alter the way your brain processes information. This will support the journey mapped out in this book and remind you of what has worked and how. Let's begin— hope is waiting.

CHAPTER 1

Positive Psychology as a Science of Hopefulness

"Life isn't about finding yourself. Life is about creating yourself."

—*George Bernard Shaw*

I often travel through Penn Station in New York City, and over the years I've seen many homeless people begging and talented musicians playing for spare change from commuters. On a particular afternoon, an exceptional violinist was playing an unfamiliar concerto that drew a significant crowd. As it did, one homeless man seized the opportunity and began begging the group for change. He would thrust his change-filled coffee cup in front of each person, shake it, and utter how he needed "just a quarter." Most of us were annoyed by his intrusive behavior—myself included.

Finally, someone simply shook his head no and pointed in the direction of the violinist. As if woken from a trance, the homeless man began to listen, swaying ever so slightly. He seemed magnetically drawn to the music, and his halting footsteps eventually brought him directly in front of the violinist. The homeless man bent over and poured the contents of his change-filled coffee cup into the open violin case. He then flashed a thumbs-up to the violinist, who responded with a deep nod of appreciation. Nearly every person who witnessed the event—myself included—reached into their wallet to take out money for both men.

To me, this transformational scene in Penn Station seemed to be an allegory. You can think of the homeless man as our negative and annoying thoughts, distracting us from appreciating something good. But when invited to notice the beauty, benefit, and blessing of the beautiful music, by giving everything he had to the musician, the homeless man received way more. His needs were unexpectedly met with abundance.

This is exactly the process with our own perception. When we shift away from distracting negative thoughts toward something positive, we get everything we need—and then some. In my own depression, when I began using positive psychology tools, for the first time the sadness lifted and I felt hope. I felt more energized and positive, which gave me more motivation for change. Since I immersed myself in understanding how hope works, my life has flourished tremendously, in ways I could not have fathomed. As you apply these principles, the same will happen for you. You are meant to do more than just survive—you are meant to thrive.

My ultimate aim is to give you tools to use when times are tough, tools that will rekindle, magnify, and engage you in life again. There is tremendous value in learning how to work with the more bitter and difficult aspects of our life, as therein lies our potential for growth. For us to feel and function better, we need to perceive and experience our struggles differently—through the lens of hope. That we can learn to do this is the promise of positive psychology. Hope is the result of believing that change is possible, and having the tools to make it happen.

Just as when building a home, shovels are used first, to dig a foundation, then a hammer and nails are used to build the walls, different tools are needed during the process of building hope.

Homebuilders and hope-builders alike need a plan, a design to guide them. The blueprint for hope is inspired by the simple fact that we can influence our future.

Psychology's Shift from Focusing on the Past to Creating the Future

In the 1960s, Martin Seligman[7] theorized that feeling helpless and giving up in one situation creates feelings of helplessness in other situations, causing symptoms of depression. Initially, he and Steve Maier researched how animals failed to escape shock after it was induced by uncontrollable aversive events. The term "learned helplessness" came from these studies and was eventually extended to how the real or perceived inability to control the outcome of a circumstance based on past "learning" was the cause of passivity. In the '60s, the understanding and technology didn't allow for investigating the nuanced elements of how the brain functioned, so it was thought that depression was the result of *learned* helplessness. Seligman's research and theory have been the dominant view of depression in psychology—until now.

In their fifty-year follow-up, the same researchers proved their initial theory wrong. Once they were able to use all the developments in brain science and biochemistry, they discovered that "Passivity in response to shock is not learned. It is the default, unlearned response to prolonged aversive events...which in turn inhibits escape."[8] This deeper understanding has us *looking forward* to gain control—not backward to unlearn what has happened.

These new discoveries explain how bad events cause us to be anxious and passive—by default. When something bad and prolonged happens, we are evolutionarily programmed to shut down. We become passive because evolution has provided us with a switch that shuts us down, to save our energy when the situation seems bad.

What this means for hope is that our very ability to *detect* and *expect* control in the *future* will pull us out of a slump. Focusing on what can be done in the future rather than on what happened in the past creates hope. In the researchers' own words: "We speculate that it is expectations of a better future that most matter in treatment."[9]

This has direct implications for where hope comes from. How well we envision what is yet to come will determine our motivation. Focusing on what's happened in the past keeps us sitting in the dark. When we concentrate on future possibilities, we can stand in the light. The pathway in the brain discovered by Maier and Seligman that regulates this future forecasting is called, appropriately enough, *the hope circuit.*

The Role of Hope in Our Lives

According to Martin Seligman, the "father of positive psychology," hope is expecting that future bad events will be temporary, specific, and manageable. Other researchers, like Charles (Rick) Snyder and Jennifer Cheavens,[10] have suggested that hope involves having a pathway to achieve goals and the agency, or motivation, to reach these goals. Still other researchers, like Barbara Fredrickson, understand hope as an exception, because unlike other positive emotions, it comes into play only when our circumstances are difficult or at least uncertain.[11] And medical researchers such as Kaye Herth[12] have found that hope happens when there is sufficient support.

No unifying theory on hope has emerged. The research findings are like the parable of the three blind men holding a different part of an elephant and then describing what the elephant looks like: each description is accurate, yet not complete. So I decided to put together the puzzle pieces from different theories and findings concerning hope. The result is a set of tools that can make hope happen.

High-hope people have a high degree of agency, the energy and motivation to bring about a change. They also have a pathway, a way to get there, and are particularly good at generating new pathways when they are met with obstacles. They are both resilient and resourceful. This is what we will be working toward in this book.

Hopefulness Does Not Discount the Negative

There are common misconceptions about hope that I want to address in this chapter. Here is the first.

Myth #1: Hope is purely positive.

Fact: Hope is the only positive emotion that needs negativity or uncertainty.

Hope requires negativity or uncertainty to flourish. It is the obstacles, the setbacks, and the disappointments that hold the emotional nutrients for growth.[13] The history of psychology has taught us much about discouraging emotions. What makes positive psychology the most rapidly developing specialty in the field is the effect positive emotions can have on the negative. By applying specific tools to activate and enhance our positive emotions, we can shake loose the grip that negative emotions can have in our lives.

Hopefulness is unique because it lives in the balance between positive and negative. As you will learn, it results from a series of decisions about how we interpret setbacks and act upon the world. Hope is a seed planted in the muck of our life that will do everything it can to find the light.

Exploration: The Thoughts That Hold You Back

One of the main features of depressed thinking is rumination. These familiar repetitive thoughts pull us into a downward spiral, robbing us of the energy to change. As we move toward the perspective shifts that lead to hope, I invite you to write down these repetitive thoughts. They hold you back, and identifying them is the first step in challenging them. You're not going to confront these thoughts just yet, but you'll want to get a sense of what you are up against.

Think about the things you want or have wanted and what is preventing you from these goals. Where are you stuck? Please turn to your journal and take time to write about this now. Believe it or not, just writing down what is bothering you has been shown to have a therapeutic effect. As you develop the tools for turning these thoughts around, we'll circle back to this in Chapter 6.

Small Efforts Can Activate Hope

Hope is not a feeling of longing for something yet being unable to make it happen. It involves the agency to change things.

Myth # 2: You either have hope or you don't.

Fact: Hope can be activated and cultivated.

Evidence shows that finding small ways to feel better activates hopeful feelings—which means that hope can be regulated, improved, and cultivated.[14] It also seems that having fewer negative feelings leads to higher levels of hope.[15]

This is a game-changer—a radically different understanding of how to introduce hope in our lives. Instead of waiting for hope to arrive and motivate us, we can do something immediately to activate it and bring it closer to our awareness. We have the power to activate hope, by using specific approaches to help us make better choices.

Your depression isn't random. There are specific reasons it exists. Depression typically grows out of worrying, and as humans we were born to worry. But about what, how often, and when we worry is unique to you, and learning to change these patterns will help release you from the grip of negativity and improve your mood. It all begins by noticing that we feel more drawn to paying attention to the negative than to the positive.

Become Aware of Seeking the Negative

In many ways, the condition of being human sets us up for negative thinking. Think about when you have something stuck in your teeth. A piece of kale, perhaps. Where does your tongue go? It goes directly to the problem and works to solve it. If you have bitten your lip, your tongue does the same thing—it is immediately dispatched to soothe the wounded area. What your tongue *never* does is hang out by your back molars, feeling how nice they are. The tongue's default mechanism is to sweep the mouth, constantly looking for problems. If something doesn't taste good, feel right, or is injured—the tongue goes on full alert, and works to resolve it. But when your tongue detects everything is okay, it doesn't do a damn thing.

Our brains work the same way. A brain is, first and foremost, a tool for survival. Its first job—like the tongue's—is to protect us from what's wrong, bad, or dangerous. The brain has evolved over centuries, developing what evolutionary scientists call a "negativity bias": we are hardwired to move away from what can hurt us.[16]

The brain is constantly assessing what is and isn't a threat. If something is a danger, the brain figures out what needs to be done. If you've ever walked down a city street with hundreds of people around, you know what happens when one person starts yelling too loud or starts a fight with someone. You go on high alert and begin assessing the situation. *Should I run away? Run toward? Stand still?* Danger dominates our concentration and concern. Our brain is in search of what's wrong, making these assessments between twenty and fifty thousand times a day.

Negative thoughts are often the essential ingredients for our success as they can motivate us to change. Isn't that the reason you got this book? Your negative thoughts, feelings, and experiences allowed you to believe that something might help. Your pain motivated the need for change and generated hope—instead of reminding you of your weakness, it summoned your strength. You can learn to summon this strength anytime you need it.

The Balancing Force of Positivity

Just like the tongue does more than protect us, the brain is designed to do more than worry. Survival and enjoyment both strive to keep us safe and happy. We need both: to push away from what can hurt us and be pulled toward what will help us grow. Only worry tips the scale too far in the direction of anxiety and depression. Focusing only on the pleasures of life makes us too vulnerable. We need an equalizing of our abilities and motives—emotional balance, like the ancient philosophies have told us all along.

What happens when you see something good? If you're like me you'll probably notice it, but you won't pay nearly as much attention as you would if you felt threatened. Someone helping a woman carry her bags will be noticed, but the screaming man yelling at a passing bicyclist will hijack our attention.

We are programmed to notice negativity, but when we continue to focus on it, a decision is being made. What causes depression is repeatedly focusing on the negative—and then getting stuck there. It emphasizes our weaknesses and erases possibility from our future.

When you are blocked from your goal and can't find a pathway to it, the disappointment causes your body and brain to react. More often than not, our first reaction is anger—blaming others for what's happened. Then we often blame ourselves. After this, we usually give up. Why bother?

These initial responses have very deep ties to our evolution. Like the tongue or brain, we are assessing a potential threat. Can this hurt us? Do we run away from the conflict? Attack it? Or will we assess the situation to come up with an idea about what to do? Although these moments may seem like a reflex, you are making an assessment, *a decision* about their potential to harm. You are making a choice about how to take action.

New research[17] shows that symptoms of depression appear to be default human reactions to bad events. This places depression in the same category as other (situational) threats where we are forced to appraise and choose a response. Just like negative events hijack our attention, causing us to appraise the threat in a situation, feeling angry, anxious, or stuck when expectations haven't been met does the same thing. Ruminating on the negativity puts our brain in a threatening situation. The result? We give up. Why waste valuable energy on a threat we are convincing ourselves can't be changed? If we persuade ourselves that the future can't be influenced by our actions, the default response is depression.

Adding Hope to Evolutionary Reactions

Where is hope in this response? Hope is another resource that is present, and it can be cultivated as a strong alternative to the other three. Fight, flight, or freeze aren't the only options. Finding hope is a fourth. Adding hope to the list offers a more accurate and complete understanding of what is possible when we are confronted with negativity or uncertainty.

Hope is what happens when another thought comes in and assesses what we can do with the situation. *Is there something I can do to make a change?* Hope doesn't deny the situation—it just defines it differently. Like when you picked up this book. You didn't deny your situation; you were simply searching for another way to look at it.

Getting angry, giving up, and feeling stuck might have more to do with reflexes than a thoughtful reaction, *but they are still the result of an appraisal.* Because of the negativity bias, when bad things happen they get higher priority. But that doesn't mean they have to dominate. If you don't challenge your thinking about something, the negativity bias is sure to keep interpreting what happened as a threat. This is what gets us stuck. We keep appraising the situation as a menace and continue to protect ourselves from it, focused on survival.

When we experience loss, have a goal thwarted, or are frightened, we assess the situation and study our pain. When this happens, one or both of the necessary ingredients for hope is activated: we feel negative and/or uncertain. While these are exactly the same triggers for fight, flight, or freeze, they also spark what is necessary for hope. When we ask ourselves, *What can I do now?*—we have an opportunity. Instead of "fight," "flight," or "freeze"—we can focus on "future." Hope is also an assessment—one of *future* possibilities. But we may need tools to help us make this shift in perception.

Exploration: Experiment with Shifting Your Attention

To illustrate how a shift in perception takes place, examine this image of a duck facing the left side of this page. Notice the duck's bill and eye.

Now slowly look over to the right of this figure. As you do, the eye of the duck becomes the eye of a rabbit facing the right side of this page. The two protruding shapes take on the appearance of the rabbit's ears. Glancing back to the left you'll perceive the duck again. Shifting to the right, you'll see the rabbit. You should be able to go back and forth between the two animals, shifting impressions according to what you focus on.

I invited you to look at this picture of a duck and you easily spotted it. But when you were invited to look at it another way, you saw something different—a rabbit. Both ways of perceiving are valid. As you were encouraged to look at the image in another, more specific way—you did. Afterward, your perception included both ways of seeing. As you changed the way you looked at it, the thing you looked at changed.

This is what we are after—a shifting perspective. Once we realize there is another way of seeing something, we then have a choice, about how it is seen. When something happens to put us in a bad mood, the world can seem barren and redundant. But when we are invited to shift our perception just slightly and asked to look at it through a different lens, something changes. We see the world differently, and can respond to it with more positivity.

What is important about this exercise is that the image you were looking at never changed—you just looked at it differently. It appeared to you differently because *you* changed your perspective. In the same way, shifting your perception can lead to seeing the world in a more hopeful way. We can't change what we're looking at, but we *can* choose our perspective. This is the essential ingredient if you want to change how you feel.

Having hope is different from having faith that something, or someone, external will come to our rescue. Instead, it gives *us* the power to change our lives—which we can continually draw on throughout our lives. This distinction is important for our sense of agency and motivation to change the way our brain works.

Myth #3: Hope is the same as faith.

Fact: Hope is when we believe *we* can positively impact our future.[18] Faith is when we believe something else will.

Seven Decisions That Generate (or Limit) Hope

Research has shown that focusing on what's wrong prevents us from seeing what's strong.[19] This brings to light another misconception.

Myth #4: Your circumstance regulates how much hope you have.

Fact: You can adjust your aspirations and goals to regulate how much hope you have.[20]

With hope, depression can become a catalyst for change, anxiety can be transformed into courage, and even trauma can be an opportunity for tremendous personal growth.[21] The key is knowing that, either way, a decision is being made about how much influence we have in creating a better future. These decisions can put us in a better place spiritually, mentally, and physically—or send us into a downward spiral.

I've observed there are seven of these decisions. Progress in making one decision facilitates other high-hope decisions. In the same way beginning an exercise program might make you more thoughtful about what you eat, initiating one good decision supports making others.

Decisions That Limit Hope	High-Hope Decisions
Seeing things as fixed and unchangeable	Seeing possibilities
Focusing on the negative	Noticing beauty, benefits, and blessings
Settling on habits of negativity	Cultivating positive feelings
Concentrating on weaknesses	Focusing on strengths
Remaining unengaged and unchallenged	Creating challenging goals
Lacking a sense of meaning and a sense of mattering in life	Finding purpose
Remaining isolated and serving only self-interests	Cherishing relationships

Like the different sounds of an orchestra that together make a harmony, each of the decisions contributes something to the whole. Thus, this book has a chapter devoted to each.

Hope Is Assessing the Future and Influencing It

Hopefulness has several features that can be developed. As positive psychologist and MacArthur "genius" Angela Duckworth has said: "*I have a feeling tomorrow will be better* is different from *I resolve to make tomorrow better*."[22]

By reading this book, you hope to learn something that changes what you feel is possible. Cultivating hope focuses on the future in a more proactive way than depression. Fight, flight, or freeze are focused on controlling the present. Hope assesses our degree of control over the future, and then chooses the optimal way to respond. While hope's essential ingredients are the same negativity or uncertainty as depression, it repurposes them toward something constructive.

Depression appears to be an evolutionary reaction to a chronically difficult situation, when we believe we have nothing left to try. We give up, shut down, and conserve whatever it is we suppose we have left, no longer interested in optimizing our future.

While negative emotions pull us into the present and the past, they, like hope, are assessing our future—but the assessment is dismissive. With depression our assessment is *Why bother?* It tells us not to put more energy into future plans.

Hope is different. Hope forecasts possibilities. While it grows out of the same dynamics that create depression, it looks at alternatives *toward* the goal, rather than retreat from it. Making better decisions about how we perceive and what we do with these dynamics moves us forward toward hope. You can get angry, retreat, give up altogether, or find hope.

One of the secret ingredients of hope is recalibration. For example, when you saw this title, *Learned Hopefulness,* you might have thought, *Yeah, right.* Or you might have thought, *Sounds interesting.* Whatever your initial reaction, you ended up with this book in your hands, and you're reading it right now. You took a step toward *possibility.* Doubtful thoughts and feelings might have made the choice harder; curious thoughts and feelings might have made it easier.

But it was the act that counted. Whether you were conscious of it or not, the act started you on a path of possibility. Other acts followed, building on each other: clicking the "buy" button, opening the book and starting to read, finding a paper scrap to mark your place, and so on. Bit by bit, without making a big deal or overthinking it, you've moved in a positive direction.

There is a "natural self" and a "habitual" self. No infant is born thinking to itself, *Why bother?* Our natural state is curiosity, wanting to learn how to grow, hoping for some influence over our future. Our interpretation of experience produces a habit of thought, and habits are decisions that can be changed. We remain stuck in our depression when we continue these thought habits, and knowing they are habits gives us the power to transform them.

Hope is coming back to a natural self—to what is already there. In positive psychology terms, our ability to change is a series of tiny steps along a cobblestone path of positive possibility. When you make a habit of hope, all the little positive choices become easy, even automatic. That is learned hopefulness.

Apply Shifts in Perspective to Imagine Anew

When we stop believing in ourselves and our goals, we don't try to make things better. Think of the times you've given up: a job, a relationship, or a condition jammed you up and caused you to dwell on what went wrong, the injustice of it, the pain. Even if giving up is the best thing, it is our assessment of the future that causes the sadness. We get depressed because we can't see how to make things better. *When negativity and uncertainty are seen as obstacles, they keep us stuck and lead to depression.*

We decide based on our assessment, and our assessment is informed by our perception. If we can look at our situation in a slightly different way, our perception changes. We can then either make modifications to how we will get to our goal, or recalibrate to a different goal to shoot for. *When negativity and uncertainty are seen as indications of a need to summon our strengths, we change our aspirations or methods.*

Each of the seven decisions in this book will require altering your perspective. Just as light passing through a prism transforms into different colors naturally, we will be filtering old habits of thought through the prism of perspective.

When we look at the world through a different lens, we can restore our natural curiosity and agency. This shift helps us make the seven decisions that lead to hope. Hope needs energy to arise. Where is that energy going to come from? If you see the glass as half empty, it's hard to find enthusiasm. Someone telling you to see it as half full typically doesn't help much. The real shift happens when you realize your glass is refillable.

According to research by Barbara Fredrickson,[23] positive emotions generate energy. Think of the last time you were out at a concert, a sporting event, or laughing with your friends. When you feel good, you are energized. We want to refill our glass with positive emotions.

Positive feelings generate the desire for what Dr. Fredrickson calls "broaden and build." Exercised regularly, the willingness to make changes, see other things differently, and challenge our perceptions takes on a life of its own, becoming effortless because of the energy it creates. In her book *Positivity*[24], Dr. Fredrickson explains that you want to use the techniques in new ways (broaden) and add new techniques to feel better (build). In contrast to the downward spiral of depression, this creates and an upward spiral of positivity.

Noticing and Activating Positive Emotions

Once a perception or a way of thinking is challenged, the possibilities need to be nourished. This is where using positive emotions becomes essential. I've found it useful to think about positive emotions in relation to time:

- the past (serenity, gratitude, satisfaction, pride, forgiveness)

- the present (interest, pleasure, savoring, awe, joy, amusement, mindfulness, and kindness)

- the future (hope, optimism, inspiration, faith)

Of course, these categories are not mutually exclusive. As an example, untangling from the past via forgiveness allows us to be more kind in the present. When we are clouded by negativity generated from a past hurt, it is more difficult to see the good in the present. In contrast, when we feel optimism, it is related to our future.

At the very core of the research into positive emotions is the study of how to activate them. Think about it this way. If you were asked to help make someone more depressed, what would you tell them to do? You'd tell them to ruminate about the things that bother them, make sure they stay isolated, listen to news about horrible things they can't do anything about, and worry as much as possible. It may sound funny, but this is a way to understand how interventions, activities, and conditions work to create a result.[25]

Positive interventions, like the ones you'll practice in this book, make us feel better, and feeling better leads to wanting more good feeling. Therefore, shifting perspective is about learning to continually seek out ways to view the world through a different lens. Through these cumulative moments, hope emerges as a natural outcome.

Feeling better about a situation is good, but cultivating hope makes life worth living. At the core of cultivating hope is attending to what we've overlooked. We are not fabricating something to be positive about, but rather, balancing out our negativity bias, which has us obsess about what's wrong. This bias can be changed when we highlight the good things already present in our life.

We pass by good things all the time without noticing them. Wonderful things happen to us, but get eclipsed by our negativity or swallowed up by our to-do list. We can correct this by shifting what we attend to—and in doing so, we change our expectations and experience.

Shifting Attention to Change Your Stories

It can be difficult to take in positivity when you're in a crummy mood—like looking for the sun when it's overcast. The sun is there, but there are too many clouds to see it. Dwelling on past wrongs can create a storm of negative thinking.

What helps is assessing what resources can be brought into the moment—deliberately trying to look at the situation in another way. If it's stormy, you need shelter and safety. Looking for resources in the present moment is essential—and it's a skill that can be learned. Activating the resources that you have immediate access to is crucial. Like the man in Penn Station who pointed the violin out to the homeless man so he too could focus on something good, gratitude is a resource that can point out our negative habits of mind.

Studies by Sonya Lyubomirsky and her colleagues have shown the power of our thoughts and actions on how we feel.[26] This is not only true of the present moment and the future—it is also true about how we think of the past. Leading psychologist Phil Zimbardo echoes this perspective when he says: "While no one can change events that occurred in the past, everyone can change attitudes and beliefs about them."[27]

How we think about our past, and the story we tell ourselves about it, is also the concern of cognitive psychologist and Nobel Prize–winner Daniel Kahnaman. Dr. Kahnaman believes that our life satisfaction is influenced by *what we remember* of the story we tell ourselves about our lives.[28] He contends that our experience is one thing and our memory of it is another. The deliberate decision to think, act, and recall in particular ways can influence our hope, happiness, and life satisfaction. Choosing to think about the better parts of our life experience will serve us better. This exercise offers you an opportunity to try out this shift in perspective.

Exploration: An Attitude of Gratitude Brightens What You Notice

Get your journal and try this out for yourself.

Step 1: List everything you can remember doing yesterday. Don't leave any-thing off—even if it was just doing chores like taking out the garbage or washing dishes. Then set this list aside.

Step 2: On a fresh piece of paper, write about that same time period through the lens of gratitude. Think back to the past twenty-four to thirty-six hours and come up with at least three things that you feel thankful for. The more specific, the better. If you're grateful because the weather was beautiful yesterday, that's good, but if you took a walk because it was nice outside and ran into a friend you hadn't seen in a while, that would be even better. You may recall things that were not on your list in Step 1.

Step 3: Look at the two lists. If you're like most people, your memory of yester-day in Step 1 was rather matter-of-fact, recalled through a habitual lens. The first list was constructed based on how your brain typically functions—with a negativity bias in place. But when looked at through the lens of gratitude in Step 2, the day becomes highlighted by positivity. A so-so day likely gets better, or a good day is enhanced. Has your overall sense of how your day went shifted?

When you were invited to look at the same day through the lens of gratitude, that created a shift in perception. You noticed events that happened but hadn't been perceived, or at least hadn't been emphasized. Once you notice the positive, your whole perception of the day shifts, in the same way that after you are invited to see the rabbit you no longer only see the duck.

Gratitude Changes Your Brain Structure

There is some very wise science behind the saying "Count your bless-ings." When we focus, acknowledge, and savor the good things that have happened, we are changing the structure of our brain. This ability for the brain to change is called *neuroplasticity*.[29] Brain science tells us that recalling these events differently not only changes our memory of what happened—it also changes the brain structure the memory is stored in.[30] Seeing things through the lens of gratitude changes the biochemistry and neural pathways in our brain. Highlighting the good stuff helps to balance out the difficult things.[31]

Once our brain has learned it can view things differently, it will start to see more positivity on its own. In the exercise, when you looked at your first list again, perhaps new possibilities arose. You may have viewed neutral or negative events with a more generous lens, and positive experiences were enhanced. If it wasn't such a good day, this exercise has likely elevated it in your memory; if it was good, you got to savor it and enhance your good feelings about it. Either way, gratitude for what is already in your life is your most immediate resource to shift your perspective toward the positive.

Even if your evaluation of the day didn't change in this exercise, you have begun the shift in your brain. In the beginning, we have to intentionally seek out gratitude and practice seeing with it. Some positive psychology practitioners have called this "hunting the good." The brain has a default mode, so we typically think and do what we did the last time. Changing the brain's default requires attention and effort. Your brain changes because your perception shifts. When you change the way you look at things, the brain you look with changes.

The good things were already there; you just had to acknowledge them. Although you were looking at the same day, another way of seeing it allowed you to view it in a new way. This brings up another misconception about hope—that it is manufactured or invented.

Myth #5: Having hope changes what we believe.

Fact: Hope is informed and primed by our beliefs.

Causes for hope are always present, we just need to believe they can be present within our experience.[32] This is why a regular gratitude practice is so important—it's an intentional effort at well-being. Altering how we view past events helps us in the present and the future. Gratitude not only changes the memory of yesterday, it also changes how you feel at the moment—and participants in studies that practice reflective gratitude, as we just did, reported a significantly more positive life.[33] Not a bad payoff for viewing your day through the gratitude lens.

Research on positive emotions shows they change our brain and body chemistry.[34] It's a choice we all have, to shine a light on the more positive features of each day and thus change our feelings, brain, and outlook. Gratitude can be generated through cognitive means such as reflection, and through expressive means such as journaling. And there is one more step that can make the experience of gratitude even more profound—telling another person.

Exploration: Share Your Gratitude with Others

When I invite people to share their gratitude with another person, the simple act of interaction is deeply energizing. People enjoy telling others about the good things that have happened to them. It stimulates an upward spiral. You could even find a gratitude partner to share with in an ongoing way.

Another way to share is to write a letter of gratitude to someone.[35] This requires a cognitive review of past events and acts that inspire gratitude, expressing it by writing it down, and interacting with another by delivering the message. I encourage you to think of those you have gratitude for and write them a note, give them a call, or go knock on their door. It's one of the best things you can do to enhance everyone's well-being.[36]

We've dug the foundation, and now we're ready to build hopefulness. Each of the seven decisions that follow are choices we can make to improve how we see and live in the world. Collectively, these decisions generate high hope. Old patterns of thought can deceive us into thinking that we don't have a choice about what we are experiencing—but we do. In the words of William James: "When you have to make a choice and don't make it, that is in itself a choice." The choices you are making and your acts of intentional well-being are powerful, because *hope is never further away than your next thought.*

CHAPTER 2

Seeing Possibilities

"Each of us literally chooses, by his way of attending to things, what sort of universe he shall appear to himself to inhabit."

—*William James*

Stacey cried throughout our first session. She shook her head and, through her tears, asked, "How could this happen?" She was forty-two and this was her first time in therapy.

Eventually, the story came out: Stacey's husband, Tom, was a lawyer. Stacey's job as a fourth-grade teacher allowed her to be home for their sixteen-year-old son and twelve-year-old daughter. They spent the holidays with extended family, had good friends nearby, and their last family vacation had been to Disney World. By every measure, life was good and moving forward—until Stacey checked Tom's work calendar on his home computer. His open online diary told his secret: he'd been having an affair for two years.

She was lost, hurt, angry, and confused, but most of all, sad. When she looked up from her mascara-streaked tissue, her eyes met mine. "What am I going to do now?" she asked.

"You're here," I said, "and for now, that is the best thing you could be doing for yourself."

"But," she said, "he's a lawyer, and he's going to hurt me financially in the divorce. Who's going to want to date a forty-two-year-old with two kids and no money?" When her next comment came, I was expecting it: "I feel hopeless."

Stacey believed that her circumstances were unchangeable, and that the changes she was facing were unavoidable. Her attitude on that first day was indicative of a fixed belief: if we think our situation is set in stone and "fixed," then there is no incentive to try. We assess our future and decide that no plan we might come up with will work. We lack the motivation to move forward because we can't see a way to get there, and we don't bother seeking support for change because we don't believe it will happen. There's a perverse sense of security in "knowing" there's no hope, that we have no power.

Yet there is another way to respond to loss. Jeannie, a first-grade teacher in Stacey's school district, was also one of my patients. The year before, like Stacey, she'd discovered that her husband, a financial consultant, was having an affair. Her boy and girl were a bit younger, but the circumstances and situation were largely the same as Stacey's. Jeannie's initial session was also informed by tears, yet she didn't ask, "What am I going to do now?" Instead, she said, "I need to figure out what I'm going to do now."

In Jeannie's statement, the essential tools of hope are present. The core difference, compared to Stacey's fixed belief that her situation was unchangeable, was Jeannie's resolve to make her future better and consider possibilities. When I met them, Stacey and Jeannie each faced an uncertain future—their sense of certainty had been wrecked when they discovered their husbands' affairs. For Stacey, stuck in a directionless, hopeless present, getting to the possibility of hope became our first goal in therapy.

For Jeannie, though, therapy began in a different place. Her situation was every bit as uncertain, painful, and unwanted. But her "I need to figure out what to do" had two elements that Stacey's "What am I going to do now?" did not:

1. *Direction:* Jeannie is standing in the present, looking toward the future.

2. *Agency:* She knows she has some choices to make, and that she wants to act.

In this way, Stacey and Jeannie had different beliefs about their future. Jeannie's statement activated hope. If we believe we can influence our future, that generates a spark of motivation, which in turn generates questions: What happens next? What support will we need? We don't know how things will turn out, but we're willing to move forward anyway.

The Difference Between a Fixed Mindset and a Growth Mindset

When we tend to hold one kind of belief over the other, we develop a mindset. A fixed mindset leads to limitations, while a growth mindset leads to possibilities. With a fixed mindset, like Stacey's, you see your abilities as set in concrete. With a growth mindset, like Jeannie's, your abilities are like clay, waiting to be formed. Their different mindsets were apparent from the words they used about their future. There is power in what we expect will happen.

Fixed versus growth mindsets have been studied by Carol Dweck and her colleagues.[37] Their work shows that a fixed mindset keeps our thoughts focused on limitations, negative interpretations, and problems. A growth mindset shines a light on possibilities and the *belief* that we have control over our talents and abilities—which allows us to engage in an effort to improve.

Another way to put it is that our mindset determines if we have an optimistic outlook or a pessimistic one. The ultimate factor in determining a successful outcome is where we focus our attention. Staying focused on limitations, negative interpretations, and problems generates the belief that our situation is fixed and unchanging. By looking toward possibilities, our thoughts shift toward seeing our abilities and talents as improvable through effort, which can change situations. This is a tangible understanding of the power hope has in our lives.

Not to Decide to Change Is a Decision to Keep Things as They Are

When we choose to limit hope by leaving things the way they are, this is a default decision—not to change it is *actively* accepting it. If we are feeling stuck and depressed, it's likely that these default decisions are keeping us that way. The plasticity of the brain makes it possible for the brain to change. However, if we don't do something different, the brain is perfectly okay with doing the same old familiar thing.

When we see things as fixed and unchangeable, we've decided that nothing we do will help the situation. We don't see the possibilities because we don't look for them. If we don't challenge the thoughts that keep us stuck, we can't harness the positive power of our brain.

But if we can find ways to search for what's possible and change how we feel in some small way, we can make a better decision and feel better. To elevate our emotions through these decisions brings us to what can be called "high hopefulness" because it moves us in an upward spiral. Our ability to choose a new outlook, rather than a familiar one, is fundamental to overcoming depression, anxiety, and loneliness.

Science has found that it's when we consider possibilities in the future that hope begins.[38] Turning attention toward our potential uses *what is yet to come* as a source of motivation.

Your Imagination Can Open Possibility

When something threatens us, it prevents us from being fully ourselves. We naturally turn toward security and safety, and all our possibilities narrow down to one thing: survival. Anything that threatens who we are evokes that same powerful, self-protective reaction. It's how we are built. And unfortunately for us, we tend to react to even potential, anticipated, or *imagined* vulnerability as if it's real.

Often what we imagine about ourselves and our situation determines how we react to it. This can keep us stuck in a protective survival mode—or it can lead to positive choices for moving forward. We can harness imagination as an antidote. When we respond to uncertainty by imagining positive possibilities rather than threats, we can change both how we feel at the moment, and how we feel about what's to come.

To become more optimistic, confront your negative thoughts while envisioning outcomes that are more positive. The dream of your future becomes your imagined reality—and research shows you will move toward it. As Peter Drucker said: "The best way to predict the future is to create it."[39] This link between envisioning a positive future and feeling the motivation to attain it creates an upward spiral, instead of the downward spiral of depression that keeps us stuck. Thoreau advised us long ago that "if one advances confidently in the direction of his dreams, and endeavors to live the life which he has imagined, he will meet with a success unexpected."[40]

Researchers have found he was right. They have demonstrated a technique that can get us started.[41] In studies, subjects who imagined a "best possible self" for three to five minutes, and wrote down their thoughts, generated a significant increase in positive affect. The findings concluded that imagining a positive future can indeed increase expectancies for a positive future.

Are you willing to invest one minute in your future? The best-possible-self visualization exercise was developed by Laura King, and many other researchers have confirmed its powerful effects.[42] I've added a component that enhances the effect, which involves taking a picture of yourself in the future.

Exploration: Best Possible Selfie

Think about a future where the best possible outcome has happened in every area of your life. Think about your career, creative endeavors, academic life, love, relationships, hobbies, health—everything. Think about what would happen in these areas of your life in your best possible future. Imagine everything working out in the best possible way.

Next, follow these steps.

Step 1: Write it all down. As you write down everything about your best possible future life, it may be tempting to drift into thinking about the difficulties, setbacks, or obstacles. But this exercise is exclusively about the future—not about the past. Imagine circumstances changing enough that a brighter future unfolds for you. You are aligning with the best possibility of yourself. Write down these future possibilities as if they have already taken place. Instead of "My house will be paid off," try "My house is paid off, and we just had a mortgage-burning party with all my friends and family."

Make it specific but not limiting. Just like when we did the gratitude exercise, specific instances will work better than vague ones. Instead of "I have a better job," try "I have a fulfilling, lucrative job where I have creative input and my coworkers value me." But don't be so specific that you limit yourself: instead of "Bill is madly in love with me," try "I'm with the right partner, feeling in love, enjoying every moment together." You are identifying the *what,* not the *how* and *who.* If you say you see yourself flying first class, don't specify the airline.

Be creative! Don't worry about grammar, spelling, or even complete sentences. The idea is to use your powers of imagination and create something that aligns with who you are and what you want to become. Have fun with it—you are creating yourself.

Step 2: Create a selfie by depicting a scene. Tear out images and headlines from magazines, grab your kids' crayons, find models from catalogs, download stuff from the Web. One of my heroes is the great neurologist and writer Oliver Sacks. I've found pictures of him that are inspiring to me and have Photoshopped images where my face is inserted onto his. This is for you—so make it something you can resonate with.

Step 3: Keep this image in a place of honor. Take a picture of it to use as wallpaper on your phone, stick it on the fridge, put it up at work, or frame it and put it in your bedroom. Make it accessible so you'll see it regularly, add to it as things evolve, and don't worry about the timeline. Activating and cultivating hope, and then keeping it accessible, is important. Studies show that depicting explicit images of achievement, known as *supraliminal priming,* actually helps people achieve their goal. Research by Tanja Bipp[43] and her colleagues demonstrated that exposure to achievement-related photographs predicted academic success—and images of overcoming difficult goals predicted even greater success.

The idea behind the exercise is to get your dream into focus, so you can work toward your goal. As the American rapper, actor, author, and entrepreneur LL Cool J says: "DDHD—Dreams Don't Have Deadlines."

Cultivating Hope Takes Deliberate Effort

Transforming negative emotions and cultivating positive emotions is a pathway to accessing our strengths. These decisions build hope in us, and this activation of hope becomes fuel—the power to facilitate and cultivate further high-hope decisions. This is an important new way of understanding how hope works.

Hope is a byproduct, a side effect of engaging in decisions that lead to positive practices. Waiting to feel more hopeful doesn't help us achieve our goals. It is our *effort* that generates hope. We shift our beam of attention toward something more positive, and that changes us. We cultivate a hopeful attitude by shifting what we focus on.

The decisions that limit hope are perspectives we habitually hold when we're feeling depressed. But these perspectives are changeable. The limiting decisions are not set in stone. Changing perspective is the aim of each decision. The process looks like this:

Limiting decisions ➔ Shift perspective ➔ Hopeful decisions

Once we shift our focus, the goals we choose become a measure of hope's impact on our life. The right kind of goals, as we will learn in Chapter 6, properly calibrated to our growth mindset and positivity, become central to sustaining our sense of agency. Achieving small, calibrated goals has been linked to higher well-being than the bigger, broader goals, because it gives us regular feedback and encouragement. A belief in attainable goals creates sustainable hope—which, in turn, also helps us to find purpose and meaning.

Hope Happens When You Reach Far Amidst Uncertainty

The power behind hope also requires something that's a bit of a surprise—uncertainty. Researchers initially believed that a specific but either very easy, or impossible, goal wouldn't be a condition for hope. But they found that people with high hope created inherent challenges, to make an easy goal more difficult. Think of Jimi Hendrix playing the guitar with his teeth or behind his back, or Mohammad

Ali winding his arm up before a punch. When the challenge is low, some people will deliberately make the task more difficult, to heighten their engagement. This is because when the challenge is too low, hope is absent. If you've ever watched a group of kids make up a game, you'll see this in action. As they master one level, they make the game harder, and thus more interesting.

As you will see along the way to learned hopefulness, goals seemingly out of reach become an activator as your persistence and determination kick in. The list of examples is endless: Walt Disney fired from *The Kansas City Star* because he "lacked imagination and had no good ideas"; *Carrie* by Stephen King rejected thirty times before it was published; Oprah fired from her job as a TV news anchor for being dull; *Zen and the Art of Motorcycle Maintenance* by Robert M. Pirsig rejected 121 times before it became a classic; *Harry Potter and the Sorcerer's Stone* rejected twelve times, and J. K. Rowling told "not to quit her day job."

We feel uncertainty when something is too easy or too hard, because uncertainty promotes self-regulation. Uncertainty creates the need to level things out. If you are convinced you cannot succeed, uncertainty is missing, so the fixed mindset blocks any hope. Challenging this belief by introducing possibilities initiates some doubt about our perspective, and in so doing introduces uncertainty. It's when our limiting belief about our future opens into possibility that hope begins.

You Can Train to Hope

You are probably familiar with René Descartes's famous saying: "I think, therefore I am." Various scholars and translators have looked at his writings, and clarification on this phrase, and determined that his complete thought was: "I doubt, therefore I think, therefore I am."[44] Doubt and uncertainty are at the very essence of being human.

When I was depressed following my divorce, I felt hopeless and didn't think there was anything I could do to feel better. I had it backward—I thought hope was supposed to find me. I thought it would come and tap me on the shoulder when it was ready. But it didn't. Finally, I realized there was something I could do to help it show up.

Are you waiting for hope to come? It's time to make a different decision. As you are learning, hope has to do with our perception of our control over what's possible. When something is uncertain, we make an assessment of what we can control; what we believe we can control is what we focus and take action on. Hope is about forecasting how we *believe* things will be for us later. We choose this belief—then we marshal our forces.

If you are focused on the floor, you are not expecting to see a work of art on the wall—so you won't. If you are looking for difficulties, that is what you'll find. When we don't deliberately look for the good things, we default to what we are used to. Because our mindset is fixed on negative experiences, that is what we'll see, feel, and react to.

To change our default perception, we have to make an intentional shift. We have to decide to challenge a fixed mindset. Not choosing to make things better is a decision to keep them the same.

Like changing channels on a TV, or going into one movie theater rather than another, our decision to focus awareness on something is a simple act. Just as what we see depends on the channel we tune into or the movie we watch, what we focus on is what we think about. If you want hope, you need to tune into the hope channel, not the helpless, overwhelmed, or depressed channels.

We can change the default settings of our brain by shifting our perceptions repeatedly until new patterns of thought and memory form. We can train our brains to tune into the hope channel. Choice after choice, tiny action after tiny action, hopefulness grows.

Focusing on What You Don't Have Keeps You from Seeing What You Have

Sometimes it's easier for other people to see how we are limiting ourselves. Jack, a writer for the local paper who taught an English class at the local community college, had been referred to one of my psychotherapy groups by his therapist. During our initial meeting, he bemoaned his string of failed relationships.

Jack wore seriously past-their-prime sneakers and a wrinkled shirt that hadn't been laundered in a while, sported an unkempt beard, and introduced a disagreeable odor into my consultation room. When he announced that he was going directly to teach his course at the college, I could anticipate the impression he was giving his students and fellow faculty, letting them know he didn't care how he was seen in the world. I couldn't help but think, *Who would want to date someone who cared so little about his hygiene?*

As our session continued, Jack complained about not being where he thought he should be in life. He had visions of being a successful writer, a full-time university professor, and marrying a lovely, supportive wife. These things hadn't happened. He explained his low mood by using a quote by his favorite writer, Hemingway, about one of his characters in *The Sun Also Rises* and then suddenly who went bankrupt "gradually." Jack recounted his last few love affairs, all of which ended with him saying: "…and then, I don't know why, she left me." He had no idea that he was the one pushing them away and seemed clueless that he was perpetuating his own misery. He needed help shifting his perceptions.

I said, "You are looking at your life in a certain way—and for change to happen, you are going to have to find the courage to challenge yourself."

"Easier said than done," Jack said.

I pointed to a small quote from *The Old Man and the Sea* I have hanging in my office, and Jack read it out loud:

"Now is no time to think of what you do not have. Think of what you can do with what there is."

"Sounds like something you'd read in a fortune cookie," Jack said dismissively. "Is that where you found it?

"The author's name is beneath it," I offered.

Jack squinted, and when he couldn't make it out, he stood up and shuffled over to the quote. Shoulders slouched, he shoved his hands deep into his pockets and glanced at the name beneath the words. He nodded and muttered: "Hemingway."

Jack needed to challenge his stuck attitude and lack of awareness about how his behavior was getting in the way of his success. What he couldn't see about himself could be easily seen by others. His expectations of himself, and his inability to see his unhelpful behavior, put him into a hole every time he thought about his situation. Instead of looking at his gifts and strengths, he was focused on what he didn't have—so he couldn't do anything with what he did have. Do you face a similar challenge?

We live in a world of paradox, contradiction, inconsistency, and conflict. There's no up without a down, no win without a loss, no trust without betrayal, no love without indifference. And yet Robert Landry, the world's leading drama therapist, has identified ambivalence as the role we most often take. He points out that the most commonly known quote in the world is "To be or not to be."[45] It doesn't get more ambivalent than that.

This perpetual ambivalence means we are always trying to decide on something—including our emotions—yet it often doesn't feel this way. We may have little choice over whether to have or not have a feeling, initially, but we do have a decision to make if we are going to continue with it. We are constantly making choices about how we feel, through a fixed lens that most of us don't know exists. Our decisions about how we should continue to feel are often deeply influenced by something outside of our awareness.

We can see how this happens in the next exploration.

Exploration: What Happens When You Focus on What You Don't Want

Think about somebody you do not like—either someone you know or someone you don't know. Someone that you find despicable, or perhaps even hate.

Step 1: Write down who they are and make a list of everything you don't like about them. Are they a know-it-all? Self-absorbed? Rude? Disloyal? Dishonest? Whatever it is, think about all the reasons for disliking them and make the list as long as you can.

Step 2: Visualize this person and notice how your body feels. Notice your emotions and listen to your thoughts.

Step 3: Look at your list. Consider whether you might have just identified your exact opposite. You have created a very thorough catalog of exactly what you've devoted your life to *not* becoming.

How can it be that our dislike of someone reveals so perfectly exactly what we'd never want to be? Someone else might think the person you've identified is just dandy. Who the person is doesn't cause the reaction you experienced—our feelings come from what we believe the person represents. Feeling the way you do toward this person was prompted by features of your character you likely weren't even aware of until now.

Your negative feelings came from a projection. Just like a projector in a movie theater, when we place a horror film in front of the light, what gets projected onto the screen of our life is horrible images. If you focus on what isn't okay, what you don't have, and what is wrong, it's like choosing to show the horror movie, and then being upset by it and blaming the movie.

If you don't like the movie, you can change it. The source of our experience comes from inside of us, not outside. There is another choice that can be made. The practice to develop is asking: "Is this decision helping?"

The Biochemistry of What We Focus On

Your *vagal tone,* which determines the ratio between your heart and respiration rate, is a measure of how well you are functioning. A healthy vagal tone is shown by a slight increase in heart rate when you inhale, and a decrease in heart rate when you exhale. What is being measured is the magnitude of the mean heart rate change from one condition to another. Vagal tone is an index of autonomic flexibility directly linked to social connectedness and psychological well-being. The research shows this type of biological flexibility allows an individual to make the most of social and emotional occasions. These gains then facilitate an "upward spiral" and higher vagal tone.

Those with low vagal tone do not take these opportunities and the social advantages are not realized. When we are lonely, we do not capitalize on the potential that comes with making a connection.[46]

It was once thought that you had either a high or a low vagal tone, and that it didn't vary throughout your life any more than your height. If it was high, you had a good immune system, good social connections, were more loving and happier, and had a host of other enhanced biological processes, like better management of glucose and more control over emotions, behavior, and attention. This is why taking a deep breath followed by a long, slow exhale helps to calm us down. It stimulates the vagus nerve (which connects our heart to our brain), which in turn helps us become more tranquil. A low vagal tone meant inflammation, anxiety, depression, loneliness, and heart attacks.

The work of Bethany Kok and Barbara Fredrickson showed that we can change our vagal tone.[47] They demonstrated that meditating on the people you love (and who love you), for about ten minutes a day for about two months, changed the vagal tone in study participants. This proved that we can significantly change our positivity and physical well-being by self-generating love.

In other words, simply changing what we think about has biochemical consequences that can deeply alter us.

Exploration: What Happens When You Focus on Positivity

To understand this more, we need to experience how our body, emotions, and thinking change when we shift focus.

Step 1: Jot down three people you admire. Again, it can be people you know or don't know. Now ask yourself, what is the common thread among them? How are these people you admire alike? Find the red thread, the common denominator among them all.

Step 2: Consider whether that common denominator is a trait, ability, or characteristic you are cultivating in your life—what you aspire to. By recognizing people we admire, we highlight *our* motivations. Others may not be so enthralled with the people you've chosen.

Step 3: Now imagine a person you love and who loves you. Hold them in your mind's eye. Notice the difference in your body when you imagine your loved person, compared to the person you despise, from the previous exercise.

The skill we're developing is recognizing that you are making a choice when you continue to think about what upsets you. You can continue to dwell on the person you think is terrible, or you could switch to thinking about the admiration or love you have for another person. "To see or not to see," as it were. This demonstrates that bad feelings or good feelings about something or someone are influenced by tinted glasses we may not know we're wearing.

A Life of Possibility Is Up to You

Barbara Fredrickson said this about her work studying positive energy and vagal tone, mentioned above: "This research shows not only that our emotions are controllable, but also that we can take the reins of our daily emotions and steer ourselves toward better physical health."[48] This is a skill that you can turn into a practice to generate hope.

As we learned in Chapter 1, hope is about expectations of the future, not about overcoming the past. In our first practice on the effects of an attitude of gratitude, we demonstrated that although we can't change the past, we can look at it differently—and then feel differently about it.

This chapter showed the power of our focus to open up possibilities for hope, to feel better about life. By imagining your best possible self, you may feel more agency to reach it. Along the way, you can improve your vagal tone by focusing your lens on the positive things you perceive—like what you admire in people, who you love, and who loves you. You've learned that shifting your way of looking at something can create a very different understanding of a situation. You've identified and challenged your mindset.

Using a positive filter is not a lie—it's a choice. Both negative and positive possibilities are there; you simply choose which one to look at. When repeated over time, the choice brings change into your body, mind, and life. Small, deliberate actions can have a cumulative effect. You choose to see the world in a more hopeful way, focused on possibility. Research has found that one thing more than any other tips the scale away from depression and toward hope: expectations.

CHAPTER 3

Noticing Beauty, Benefits, and Blessings

"The question is not what you look at, but what you see."

—*Henry David Thoreau*

Couples rarely come in to therapy for a tune-up. They usually wait until the axle is broken, or the engine has fallen out.

When Kate and Sam came to me, they were somewhere in between. Nothing catastrophic had happened, but things were headed in the wrong direction. They seemed to mostly ignore or avoid each other daily, and their sex life had been steadily dwindling. They buried themselves in their work, their exercise, and their children's successes. Their youngest son was about to launch into the world, which meant that Mom and Dad would now have to face each other. It was time for them to figure out their third act and enjoy the rest of their lives. The problem? They'd stopped talking to each other.

A year earlier, Kate had taken a new position in her company, with the status and pay raise she deserved. For the first time in her career she was making more money than Sam, who felt trapped in a job where there was no room to move up. When Kate came home excited each night and wanted to talk to Sam about what she was doing and learning, Sam nodded and feigned interest, but the moment he could, he would lose himself in the TV or go off to read alone. After a few months, Kate stopped talking about her excitement, and they steadily drifted apart. Then, as is often the case, there was an inciting incident that triggered them to seek treatment.

> Kate leaned forward. "We were driving together, and at a stoplight, a procession of four black limos passed through the intersection."

> Sam said, "The question came right out of my mouth— 'I wonder whose funeral it is?'"

> Kate added, "At the very same moment, I said, 'I wonder whose wedding?'"

> "I remember looking at Kate in astonishment and thinking, how could she be so absurd as to think it was a wedding?" Sam said. "I think that was when we both realized we were in trouble."

> "I had this horrible feeling in my gut when he said 'funeral,'" Kate added. "That's the world he is living in—that's the world he is waking up to every day."

Whether the four limos were going to a funeral, a wedding, or on the way back from the car wash, the perception, label, and reaction toward the same event were as opposite as they could have been. It was as if Sam were showing the movie from his mind, entitled *Endings,* while Kate projected her movie, *Beginnings.*

Our Internal State Determines Our Experience

As the Talmud says, "We don't see things as they are. We see them as we are." How we see and respond differently to the same object has been the subject of philosophy and psychology for a long time. In the previous chapter, you saw how our experiences color the lens through which we look at life. Over time, we may no longer even realize that we are watching a certain movie from our mind or looking at the world through tinted glasses. We just accept that that's the movie we have to watch. Just as the explorations of who you despise and who you admire showed, our experience and attention inform our reactions.

Learned hopefulness is continually shifting perception toward something more hopeful. Shifting perspective is the fundamental skill for each of the seven decisions. Once we realize there is another way of seeing something, we have a choice as to how it is perceived. When something happens to put us in a bad mood, it's like our brain telling us to look at the world as if it were barren.

But when we are invited to shift our perception just slightly and look at it through a different lens, something changes. We see the world differently, with more positivity, and respond to it in kind. What you were looking at never changed—you just looked at it differently. You changed your perspective. This leads to seeing the world in a more hopeful way. We can't change *what* we see, but we can choose *how* we perceive it. The willingness to do this is essential if you want to change how you feel.

Have you ever been going through a difficult time and heard lyrics of a song jump out at you because they were so relevant to your situation? Our inner world is constantly informing not only what and how we see, but also what we hear and feel. You may have heard that song a thousand times, but now you hear it differently. Our internal state creates not only an expectation of *what* we will pay attention to but *how* it is interpreted.

What Do You Expect to See?

Our thoughts form our perspective of the world because they create an expectation. Optimists and pessimists both cultivate patterns of expectations. Our experience is informed by what we *expect* to attend to.

It's almost as if we are responding to a form of self-hypnosis. Research about hypnosis shows how powerful expectations are. In one study, subjects were hypnotized and told they were going to be touched very briefly with a hot coal. The researchers then touched the subjects with an ice cube. Immediately the participants formed a *blister* where they were touched.[49] Anticipating something bad was going to happen put them in a state where they felt they had to protect themselves—even when there was no need to—and there were consequences. And the power of expectation works both ways. Under hypnosis, subjects allergic to various substances can inhibit a reaction when told they are not affected.[50]

In these studies, the stimulus was perceived differently, based on what was expected. An ice cube can cause a blister if it is expected to burn us, and an allergic reaction can be neutralized if the allergen is perceived as harmless.

What has emerged from the research and practice of positive interventions is that they are cumulative. We learn to continually seek out a way to view the world through a different lens. The goal is to accumulate moments in which hope emerges as a natural outcome.

To Get Unstuck, First Notice That You're Stuck

You've probably experienced that hopeless feeling of being stuck with a recurring, ruminating negative thought. Some event triggers a negative loop that becomes more and more difficult to shake. When our negative emotions hijack us, it keeps our rational side from making better decisions on how to think, feel, and act.

Stopping this is a good beginning. This is what we've been learning with the exercises so far; they've been aimed at untangling you from old patterns so you can see overlooked possibilities and unrealized potential. If you've been doing these exercises, you are likely to be feeling a bit more hopeful.

To turn these insights into an ongoing change in your perception, you first have to believe that a change is possible. To believe that a change is possible, you need to know that how you are looking at something is a choice—a decision is being made. This is what we practiced in the previous chapter.

Now you're ready to bring your skills up to the next level. It's one thing to observe, change perception, and challenge your negative thoughts—but quite another to positively influence your thoughts, feelings, and perceptions. When you learned how to drive a car or ride a bike, the skills needed to slow down and stop were different from those required to change direction and pick up speed. Slowing down and stopping won't get you to your destination. In the same way, slowing down and stopping a depressed mindset isn't the same as being happy. We need to learn other skills too.

Now we are going into the very heart of understanding how thoughts change. *They change when they are noticed.* This is at once an ancient secret and the most exciting new topic for research. Becoming mindful of our thoughts and actions may be the most direct way to initiate hope.

Catch Your Thinking, to Open Space for a Choice

Many forms of psychological treatment and spiritual practices begin with an invitation to challenge our perceptions: logo therapy, rational emotive psychotherapy, cognitive behavioral therapy, acceptance and commitment therapy, resilience training, positive psychotherapy, and psychodynamic therapy, as well as spiritual practices like A Course In Miracles, Buddhism, and various forms of meditation. Each of these questions what we are thinking and how we are viewing a situation, reaction, or perception.

This challenge awakens the possibility of choice. In turn, knowing that we have a choice encourages and supports hope for the future. A powerful quote, often attributed to Viktor E. Frankl, but first expressed by psychologist Rollo May in 1963, captures this challenge: "Between stimulus and response, there is a space. In that space is our power to choose our response. In our response lies our growth and our freedom."[51]

This space is the crucial element behind our power to choose. Yet defining what precisely this space is, and how to access and nurture it, has been unexplored by science until now.

Dispositional mindfulness (DM) is a keen awareness and attention to our thoughts and feelings in the present moment.[52] Research shows that the ability to engage in this intention has many physical, psychological, and cognitive benefits. When we can react to our inner experience with awareness, in a nonjudging and nonreactive way, that creates a profound shift in how we function.

Before we go on, I want to dispel a common misperception about mindfulness practice, which was expressed by a client of mine named Roseanne.

"Nonjudgment and nonreaction?" Roseanne said, wrinkling her nose. "I'm not going to turn into one of those crunchy granola types with no personality, sitting on the floor in pretzel pose, am I?" Roseanne clearly didn't like the idea of learning these skills. "I like feeling my feelings. If I don't have a reaction, I'm just going to be boring."

"It's not about not having feelings," I explained. "It's about having enough distance between you and your experiences that you have a choice about how—or if—you respond."

Roseanne let herself try the methods I had taught her. Within two weeks she reported back. "Something has definitely changed," she began. "I'm able to watch myself, watch my thoughts. It's like I've taken a half-step back from everything—I'm more relaxed, I feel more in control of myself. I'm more hopeful."

"Sitting like a pretzel yet?" I teased.

"No, but I *have* developed a fondness for granola." She smiled.

You may think observing with awareness sounds a lot like mindfulness meditation—the Buddhist practice of mindfulness, introduced to the Western world as a form of preparing for a compassionate life and developing deeper understanding and wisdom. This style of meditation was intended by Buddhists to be a way of conscious living. But in the West, the practice is considered more of a means to an end: you'll be calmer, have lower blood pressure, better relationships, and less stress if you are more mindful.

DM is different because, while we do experience those benefits, it refers to being more conscious as we go through our moment-to-moment, day-to-day lives.[53] Mindfulness, when viewed in this way, is a quality of our life—a trait, not a state we enter into during meditation practice.

The science now surrounding DM and what I'll call *applied consciousness* may be at the very root of how we maintain hope, perseverance, and mental health. DM has been shown to change psychopathological symptoms such as depression and anxiety. It is positively linked to adaptive thought processes, and better emotional processing and regulation. All of this comes not from changing how we think, but from being aware of what we are thinking in a nonjudgmental way.

Here is just a sample of the research outcomes from nearly a hundred studies of DM.[54]

- Lower levels of perceived stress
- Lower use of avoidance coping strategies
- Fewer depressive symptoms
- Less anxiety
- Improved functioning in borderline personality disorder
- Reduced post-traumatic stress disorder (PTSD) symptoms
- Improved adaptive coping strategies
- Reduced rumination
- Less catastrophizing about pain
- Diminished neuroticism
- Improved executive function
- Decreased impulsivity
- Increased emotional stability

This is an impressive list, given that all we are doing is learning to have a nonjudging awareness of our thoughts and actions. This means that even before we attempt to change our thoughts, there is value—enormous value—in simply noticing them.

Why would noticing our thoughts have such a big effect? Because exercising this skill strengthens the essential practice of *self-regulation*. This is the secret behind each of the seven decisions. When you work on developing self-regulation through DM, you are strengthening your ability to choose what you pay attention to.[55]

According to the definition put forth by Jon Kabat-Zinn, a leading figure in the research behind mindfulness meditation, "Mindfulness means paying attention, in a particular way: on purpose, in the present moment, nonjudgmentally."[56] This definition works well for DM too.

Exploration: Becoming Mindful of Your Experience

I have found that three guidelines tend to open up the space between stimulus and response and give us an awareness of our thoughts.

Step 1: Notice what you notice. Become aware of what you notice through your senses. In your journal, write down what you see first, and then focus on what you are hearing, from the outside in. What are you seeing, hearing, and feeling right now—outside of you, and in your body? Write everything down as best you can. Move your attention around, from your feet to your shoulders, to the in and out of your breath. Write down what you are aware of experiencing, nonjudgmentally. Even if you have a negative feeling, don't judge it—you are simply noticing what you notice.

Step 2: Observe what's vivid. Next, consider what stood out for you the most. Was it the cold in your toes? The smell of jasmine from outside? How rapid your breath was? Be curious about what captures your attention and write it down. Eventually, you can take this practice out into the world. Is there a beautiful sunset? A terrific-smelling restaurant? A warm breeze? When something vivid happens—pay attention to it. Savor it, and extend your experience of it by capturing it in your journal, under the title: WHAT'S VIVID.

Step 3: Catch yourself thinking. As you bring those first two practices into your daily life, become aware of your thoughts. What are you thinking about? What are you feeling? Remember, you're not making good or bad judgments—just observations. As you begin your practice, you might want to enter these moments in a note on your phone when they happen.

Enter these observations in your journal each day for a week, then continue to try noticing them regularly. The goal is to be mindful of what is happening as it is happening. Next, keep journaling and noticing for the next month.

The exercise of DM is the beginning of an ongoing process, and is designed to become a new habit as you cultivate hope. It allows just enough light to come into a situation to remind us that we have the power to choose. The space between perception and response becomes more evident once we can see the gap. DM is an invitation to widen that gap, merely by noticing it exists.

Subtle Awareness Is the Basis for Shifting Perception

At any given moment, there is a you both having an experience and interpreting that experience. This is the first awareness. By noticing what you notice (as the Beat poet Allan Ginsberg said),[57] you both detect what you are experiencing, and become aware of your reaction to it. You become aware that there is a stimulus, your perception, and a response—your reaction. Mindfulness/DM helps you notice your thoughts and feelings as you are going about your day, creating the power to choose how or if you'll take action.

This subtle sense that there is a you having an experience creates empowerment. Just as nuclear energy is created spontaneously when one atom is divided into two, we are energized when our self can separate from our thoughts. This effort to self-regulate strengthens our ability to direct our thoughts and emotions. As the sense of self develops, so does our skill to direct our thoughts and feelings—particularly about the future.

Research has shown that the spark coming from greater self-realization through DM generates hope and grit. Even before a decision is made about how to interpret an experience, these two powerful character traits are created as a byproduct of self-regulating. We strengthen who we are when we acknowledge the space between an event and our observation of it. It gives us the power to choose how to respond.

When your reaction is disturbing, you can begin to widen that space and invite some distance between you and your experience. Again, the goal isn't to change what you are experiencing, but rather just to begin to see it nonjudgmentally. Negative experiences often hijack our attention. Being able to step back from them via DM gives us power over them.

These techniques are our training wheels. They've helped us to get the idea. But now we are ready to try and balance ourselves, and this type of balance requires a more subtle awareness. Remember the joy you felt when you no longer needed training wheels? You developed an internal understanding of what was required to slow down and stop your bike, along with a sense of power, because you knew how to get somewhere. DM is the balancing factor, the essential tool for navigating your life.

Seeing Challenges as Opportunities

Helen Keller offered a perspective on the difficulty experienced when a door closes in our life: "When one door of happiness closes, another opens; but often we look so long at the closed door that we do not see the one which has been opened for us." She should know—she was the first deaf-blind person to earn a bachelor of arts degree, and her autobiography about her teacher Ann Sullivan was turned into a major motion picture, *The Miracle Worker.*

When something bad happens to us, we are filled with dread, uncertainty, and, quite often, pessimism. The difficult experience leads us to feel negatively about our future. However, our own history, when viewed through a different perspective, changes how we interpret difficulty.

Eric, a college senior, took a train to visit his girlfriend at another college. When he arrived, she was there at the station waiting for him—only to tell him that she was breaking up with him. When she left, Eric pleaded with the train representative to change his ticket so he could return immediately. She did, and once on the train he sat in a quiet area and began to cry. Station by station, the train filled up, until a young woman took the seat next to him. After a while, she asked if he was okay, and his story unfolded. One year later they were engaged.

The following exercise deliberately looks at negative events in our life, but does so through a lens that reveals how these events may have helped us transition. It helps us see negativity from a different vantage point, by reviewing instances in our life that initially seemed hopeless—but that turned out better than we could have imagined.

Exploration: When New Possibility Results from a Loss

This exercise was researched and developed by Dr. Tayyab Rashid, one of the lead developers of positive psychotherapy, along with positive psychologist Martin Seligman. It can help you understand how darkness can shift to light in your own life. Research shows that feelings of hope and optimism result from reframing past experiences.[58]

Step 1: Write about three moments in your life when a negative event led to unforeseen positive consequences. Important things were lost, but other opportunities presented themselves that otherwise may not have. You could have closed the door, or it could have been closed on you. The important thing is that the second door could not have opened unless the first one closed.

Step 2: Reflect on your examples. In your journal, write about the circumstances that surrounded the event. If something like that happened now, would you respond differently? What positive thing(s) emerged? Were there actions you took that helped bring about the positive development?

This is a great way to learn hopefulness. We see how dark situations in our lives transformed into something positive. Something not working out on one level can be the catalyst for circumstances that are much better than what was lost.

As you review these life changes, the sting of what once felt overwhelming shifts, and what was previously so painful has opened a door to something better. Taking this broader perspective softens our negative experiences going forward. Instead of seeing only the challenges, we now know firsthand that other difficulties turned out better than expected. Our troubles become part of the fabric of growth. As the Buddhists say: "No mud, no lotus."

Earlier, you learned that changing perspectives on a situation is possible. In this chapter, you've extended this to recognize how thoughts, feelings, and experiences are self-perceived and what you notice determines what you expect in life. Paying attention and becoming aware in a nonjudgmental way is both preparation and motivation. The effort to self-regulate your experience generates hope and grit. Noticing what is happening gives you distance, drive, and the agency to make decisions about how to respond. What you notice will determine your expectations of life—and your experience.

Noticing the changeovers we've had shifts the focus from what went wrong to what might be next, keeping the emphasis on the big picture. It helps to loosen the tightness of the grip our difficulties exert in trying to capture our attention. When we learn that a bad experience can initiate something grand, it gives us hope and upgrades our expectations.

You've taken off the training wheels and learned how to ride. Now it's time to put on your helmet. Our next chapter is about cultivating positive feelings. Once you learn to ride this new bike, you'll want to go fast.

CHAPTER 4

Cultivating Positive Feelings

"The way to overcome negative thoughts and destructive emotions is to develop opposing, positive emotions that are stronger and more powerful."

—*Dalai Lama*

In a matter of weeks, Suzanne's typically serene life—working part-time at the bookstore, enjoying vacations with her husband, and babysitting her grandchildren—was turned upside down when she was diagnosed with pancreatic cancer. The aggressive chemo treatments made her beautiful auburn hair fall out in a month. She was too fatigued to babysit or work at the bookstore. These rapid changes led her to feel hopeless and powerless, which caused her family to encourage her to go to therapy.

She wore a wig to our session and focused on what she had lost, what she was missing.

"These are real losses," I told her, "and I'd be worried if you weren't sad and upset by them."

She was taken aback; she thought that, as a positive psychologist, I would try to talk her out of her bad feelings. But that was the furthest thing from my mind. I honored these feelings and noted them as essential. She had been preparing to defend them, but the fight was over before it began.

Suzanne described her loss of hope. "All the things I enjoy doing have been taken away from me," she explained. "I've lost all hope of being able to do any of them again."

Notice Suzanne said she had lost *all* hope for doing *any* of her activities again. These are absolutist statements, which revealed to me that her mind was warping the situation. Whenever this happens, it indicates black-and-white thinking. Absolute negative thinking will produce an avalanche of negative emotions, fueled by their own chemical reactions. The all-or-nothing approach meant it was time to introduce gray and beige.

The Biochemistry of Negative and Positive Thinking

When you repeatedly think about what went wrong, or what makes you anxious or angry, you are putting yourself in a continually high-alert condition—and a biochemical nightmare is happening because of it. Barbara Frederickson's research has demonstrated that the resulting negative emotions produce the fight-or-flight response, activating the body to do what it has to do to survive. The anxiety is functional, and our focus narrows to concentrate on saving our life.

This is why we have a negativity bias. We need to be prepared to survive at any time, and when we do feel threatened, cortisol, a steroid hormone produced by the adrenal gland, is released to help. It is meant to be a short-term solution to an immediate problem. It increases blood sugar to give us energy, suppresses the immune system, and metabolizes other sources of energy such as fat, protein, and carbohydrates. It also decreases bone formation, which can have an impact on children growing up in a stressful household.

Robert Sapolsky from Stanford University has written about this in his book *Why Zebras Don't Get Ulcers*.[59] Because humans can think about past and future events, we can activate—through thought alone—our body's perception that we are in a crisis situation. We worry about the mortgage, our job, our relationship, and this gets our body ready to survive—not to thrive.

Although research has shown that negative thoughts and feelings are stronger than positive ones, if you focus on what brings you joy, or what you have gratitude for, everything changes. Positive emotions send a different signal, and our body chemistry changes. We produce more oxytocin—the bonding hormone that gets released during physical intimacy or when a mother holds her baby.

Dr. Frederickson has identified ten forms of positivity: joy, serenity, interest, hope, pride, love, amusement, awe, gratitude, and inspiration.[60] Her lab has looked at what happens in the body when these forms of positivity are activated, and has found that positive emotions stimulate creativity, resilience, and well-being.

Even small experiences of positive emotion can work in this way. This can take the form of a recalibration, an adjustment to what you might have been hoping for. For Suzanne, this meant that instead of hoping for the diagnosis to be wrong, she could instead hope to be strong enough to babysit for an hour, and to return to her job for two hours. This made hope more accessible to her.

With realistic goals to focus on, Suzanne spoke to her daughter and employer about getting their support for attaining them. Almost instantly her mood improved. She had agency, a pathway, and encouragement from others toward her ambitions to her doctors that to meet these goals she would need their help managing her fatigue. The team made some changes in her treatment to accommodate her, which allowed her to feel strong enough to reach these goals within a month. Suzanne felt genuine pride and joy from this achievement. Not only did her mood improve during the process, but the success of these milestones also gave cause for celebration with the people who loved and supported her.

When she focused on what she had lost, she also lost hope. When she focused on what she could control and mobilized her immediate resources—she thrived.

Exploration: Thinking Affects Your Body

To understand the difference, try this experiment. Imagine you have a lemon in front of you that is ripe and you can smell it in the air. Then imagine you cut this lemon with a knife and the smell gets stronger. Now imagine you pick up half of the lemon and take a huge bite out of it, holding it in your mouth.

If you are like most people, your mouth will produce saliva—even though the lemon is only in your imagination. You were able to change your body chemistry by focusing your thoughts in a particular way.

Triggering an Upward Spiral with Positive Emotions

The opposite thing happens when we introduce positive emotions. In Chapter 2, you were introduced to vagal tone and the idea that regularly thinking of someone you love and who loves you can create a powerful and long-lasting effect on the body. This research changes the way we think about health and well-being, by allowing self-generated positive emotions to activate social connections, which in turn stimulate positive emotions, resulting in improved vagal tone and health. They all influence one another in a self-sustaining upward spiral.

This is where hope fits in. When you make an effort to do something positive, reflect on your gratitude, catch yourself thinking negatively, or imagine a better future, you are stopping the downward phase and giving the upward spiral a chance to start.

The important thing is to realize that this is a choice you have. Every moment offers you the ability to shift your thoughts away from negativity. Once you can do this, the upward spiral of connecting to others and having more positive emotions begins.

If you are brave enough to believe that a positive change is possible, and courageous enough to work on recalling past gratitudes, future expectations, and being more dispositionally mindful, the upward spiral begins on its own. If you put in a little bit of effort, to make a different choice about how you think of the past and present, you are cultivating the habits of positivity. This then helps you set better intentions for yourself about what's to come, in turn setting the stage for changing pessimism into optimism.

The Wide-Ranging Effects of Optimism

How do you explain the events that happen in your life? Optimists exaggerate the good and minimize the bad. Pessimists do precisely the opposite. These represent different defaults—different decisions you make about how you see the world. Each way of seeing creates a powerful expectation about the future. These expectations either help you thrive, or limit how you live your life. They are forged by the degree to which you believe you can exert control over future outcomes.

The key to understanding the difference is something called *explanatory style,* or how we explain positive and negative events in your life. These styles are often referred to as the three Ps.[61] Pessimists perceive negative events this way:

- Permanence—when something bad happens, the feeling will last forever

- Pervasive—the event will affect all areas of our life

- Personal—we alone are at fault

A pessimist responds to setbacks helplessly, views negative events as permanent and as compromising everything they do, and feels personally responsible—so the situation is out of their control to change.

Optimists explain the same negative event a different way, as neither permanent nor pervasive, and don't take it personally. Instead, they view it as a temporary hurdle, an isolated occurrence, and they see how it is controllable. This cheery outlook is more than a pleasantry—it can make you more immune to depression, with better physical health and greater, more sustainable potential for achievement. Here are just some of the results research has shown can come from optimistic thinking[62] :

- A longer, happier life
- Fewer symptoms of depression
- Lower levels of stress
- Better cardiovascular health
- Lower risk of Alzheimer's disease
- Higher levels of well-being
- More positive emotions
- Greater resilience and coping skills during difficult times
- Greater productivity
- More compassion
- Greater kindness
- Fewer negative thoughts
- Better sleep

Even when *good things* happen for a pessimist, these outcomes don't happen. This is because positive events are believed to be temporary, to be limited to one situation, and to have nothing to do with them personally. For pessimists, good things don't stick, whereas the bad things in life are long-lasting, with far-ranging implications. This difference profoundly influences expectations, which in turn lead to a distinct outcome.

Consider a pessimist, Kerrie, who gets an "A" in a course she is taking at the university. She sees the good grade as a temporary fluke—it won't happen again; it's not permanent. The good grade was only in one class and on one quiz, so it has no far-reaching impact. Kerrie would attribute it to the lucky fact she had read the right material—in other words, it wasn't something she controlled, so it wasn't a personal victory for her.

But if Kerrie fails the test, it's because she isn't smart (permanent), it will ruin her GPA and chances of completing her degree (pervasive), and it will prove she is a bad student, so there is no way to improve (personal). The negativity stays with her.

Linette, an optimist, gets an "A" and believes just the contrary. She anticipates getting good grades in the future (permanent), having her grades influence her career (pervasive), and takes credit for it happening because she put in the effort to study (personal). The positivity sticks.

If she fails a test, Linette attributes it to something temporary (like not getting a good night's sleep), dismisses it as not her usual performance (not pervasive), and thinks it happened because of something outside of her control (like the dorm fire alarm went off in the middle of the night and she couldn't get back to sleep).

The core difference between optimists and pessimists is how they think good and bad events will impact their future. From the very beginning, pioneers in mental health have seen hope as an essential ingredient that helps people feel better. Freud himself thought his patients' "expectations, colored by hope and faith" during the treatment process mostly explained its success or failure. Karl Menninger viewed hope as the essential ingredient of healing and encouraged psychology practitioners to study it. More recently, Irvin Yalom, the celebrated existential and group therapist, identified instillation of hope as a crucial factor in the therapeutic process.[63]

What Do You Want in Life?

People with high hope,[64] a frame of mind we've been moving toward with our explorations, have been shown to have better[65]:

- Psychological adjustment

- Academic performance and achievement

- Physical health and wellness

- Athletic performance

- Coping skills for illness and loss

- Social-emotional problem-solving

- Interpersonal relationships

Consider the list I shared earlier about the health effects of optimism. When taken together, these lists of attributes for optimistic and high-hope thinking can offer you motivation to cultivate an outlook that benefits you. Now that you know that your belief and expectation about what's going to happen influences the outcome, let's explore a way of developing a more positive outlook.

Becoming a better you, as you are learning, takes some work. As we go, you've been altering your perception and making changes in how you look at things, act, and recall elements in your life.

Now, to cultivate positive feelings on a regular basis, you can engage a benevolent side of yourself to dialogue with when you're in a negative place. This will allow you to internalize all your new skills so you can easily access them. A compassionate, benevolent self is something you can update and develop throughout your life. Just like we run software updates on our computers and cell phones, we can use positivity practices to update ourselves when we learn new ways to enhance hope and life satisfaction.

Embodying a Benevolent Self

Self-compassion can help you overcome self-criticism, which is a deep inner expression of pessimism. You know that inner voice that tells you you're not good enough, can't do it, aren't strong enough, and so on? This is negative self-talk, which we will get more deeply into in Chapter 6. It will grow arms and legs—and determine the direction of your life—if it isn't challenged. This voice expresses the ruminating thoughts researchers consistently find underlying depression. My guess is, if you are reading this book, you know something about having to cope with these messages.

In the face of self-criticism, reliving failures, and dwelling on personal shortcomings, you can cultivate a positive, nurturing attitude toward yourself. Researcher Kristin Neff has consistently shown that the higher our capacity for self-compassion, the greater our well-being.[66] New research from China shows that hope is an important factor linking self-compassion to increased life satisfaction. In other words, when we treat ourselves benevolently, hope strengthens—which leads us to feel better about life in general.[67]

You can develop self-compassion to nurture yourself even in the middle of a storm of negative self-criticism. How? By becoming your own best friend. Treat yourself the way a good friend would treat you. Talk to yourself in a kind way, responding to your inner critic with the type of loving attention a close friend would give you.

Exploration: Consult Your Kind Self

How we act changes how we feel. To develop your self-compassion, use a simple role-reversal method with an empty chair. Please give this a try now and write your reactions in your journal immediately afterward. Some people choose to record these sessions.

Set up two chairs across from one another. They can be the same or different, and as close or as far apart as you like. One chair will be the seat of your negative self, and the other chair will be where your inner friend sits.

Step 1: Sit in the negativity chair and let yourself speak—out loud—some of the negative thoughts or self-criticisms that you tend to have or have had in the past. In the other chair across from you is the you who is benevolent, a loving observer. Imagine that this kind part of you has your best interests at heart and is listening compassionately. Like a good friend, this kind self can ask questions or offer observations.

Step 2: When you're ready to shift roles and let your compassionate side speak, get up, switch chairs, and speak from this reversed role. Your kind self might ask why you are having a certain feeling or ask to hear more about something your negative self expressed.

Step 3: Reverse roles—and chairs—as many times as you feel is necessary. Always start and end in the chair of your negative self. Afterward, be sure to journal what you can remember of your dialogue and your reactions.

Note: If you have difficulty with mobility, while you can use an empty chair across from you and imagine the response, it's of most benefit to somehow physically move positions. People in wheelchairs can set up empty chairs across from each other and then roll next to them, back and forth, to dialogue. This embodied act of switching back and forth facilitates the process.

Two or three times a week, I have these discussions with my benevolent self. I'm still stunned at the wisdom, insight, understanding, and deep compassion this part of me has for my pain. Over the years I've found students become much more resilient and trusting of the negative part of themselves as their self-compassion develops.

People have described the process in many ways, but one that comes up again and again is that it's like a mother holding a squirming infant. The mother holds the baby long enough to let it self-soothe and self-regulate. In this exercise, you are learning how to hold yourself with this same kindness.

While you can hold this dialogue in your head, I find it's much more powerful to draw on the technique of role reversal, and actually enact these opposing sides of yourself. The strong impact that results from this is known as *embodied cognition*—a way of changing our thinking through action.[68]

Let's look at how this works, and perhaps even give you some ideas for how to take embodied cognition further. One study looked at what happens when we change how we use the muscles in our face. They found that when people were asked to put a pencil between their teeth—lengthwise, to simulate a smile—they comprehended pleasant sentences faster than unpleasant ones. Engaging the muscles of a frown by holding a pencil only with their lips had the reverse effect.[69]

In another study inspired by the "as if" principle,[70] researcher Sara Snodgrass asked people to take a three-minute walk in one of two ways. Half of the group took long strides, swinging their arms, and held their head up high. The other half took short strides, shuffled along, and watched their feet. The people taking long strides reported feeling significantly happier than those who shuffled along.

Embodied cognition regards action as something that enables perception. Findings show that how we act can influence our thoughts and feelings, making our ability to change a two-way street. We call this type of relationship bidirectional. It means we can change our perception about a situation—in changing our belief, we change how we act. Or changing our actions can foster a change in our beliefs. In the 1981 study behind the book *Counterclockwise,* Harvard psychologist Ellen Langer took this concept a step further when she created a time machine.[71] She brought eight men in their seventies to a converted monastery in New Hampshire that had been completely transformed back into the year 1959: Ed Sullivan on a black-and-white TV, Perry Como on the radio, and books and magazines from the year. The aged men—all with arthritis, stooped and needing canes—lived there for five days, told by Langer to actually try to be the person they were in 1959. Their dexterity, grip strength, flexibility, hearing, vision, memory, and cognition were measured at the outset.

They were treated as if they were younger—for example, they had to carry their belongings upstairs by themselves. To add the factor of expectation, Langer told the men, "We have good reason to believe that if you are successful at this you will feel as you did in 1959."

It worked. After the five days, they were tested again and compared to a control group who had come to the monastery and told only to reminisce, but not to act as if it were actually 1959. After only five days the men from the time machine were more agile, had greater manual dexterity, sat taller, and had better vision. Independent judges even said they looked younger.

Acting in specific ways changes who we are. Here are ten proven ways that embodied cognition can be used on a daily basis to change how you think and feel.

1. **Smile.** Believe it or not, it is that simple. Studies show that when you use the muscles in your face to create a smile, you'll actually feel better.[72] Try it. It feels odd the first few times, but the result is immediate, and it seems to instantly short-circuit negative thinking.

2. **Flex your muscles.** Tensing muscles increases willpower.[73] Making a fist or gripping a pen has been shown to help cope with pain, keep from overeating, and be able to focus better.

3. **Use your nondominant hand.** Dieters did better when they ate using their nondominant hand, because it made them more mindful. When we consciously break our old habits, we can make better decisions.[74]

4. **Start small.** We will talk more about setting micro-goals in Chapter 6, but for now start to tackle larger tasks (cleaning the basement, writing a report, paying the bills, etc.) by devoting only a few minutes to the chore. This changes the habit of procrastinating. Instead of delaying taking action by avoiding what is undesirable, by making the time very brief you can "act as if" you're interested in what you are doing.[75]

5. **Sit up straight and cross your arms.** Studies show that you can increase your persistence when you change your posture and fold your arms.[76] Subjects who did this during difficult tasks were able to keep at them for twice as long as those who didn't adopt these positions.

6. **Power walk and power pose.** You may have heard about Sara Snodgrass's power walking to increase your self-esteem, but fifty-five studies have recently confirmed that striking a "power pose" (think Wonder Woman)—as made popular by Harvard researcher Amy Cuddy—can increase your self-esteem and boost your confidence.[77] How we hold our body does indeed affect our mind.

7. **Sit softly.** Studies out of MIT suggest that those who sit in hard chairs when they negotiate are more inflexible than those sitting in soft chairs.[78] Better negotiations happen in a physically comfortable environment.

8. **Wash your hands.** Researchers studying what has been called the "Macbeth effect" have found that you may be able to wash away your sins.[79] Believe it or not, people who've engaged in immoral acts or behaviors will actually feel less guilty when they clean their hands afterward.

9. **Give yourself a nod.** Notice when you are nodding to what is being said—it means you're more likely to be in agreement. Being mindful[80] of your nodding can also help you notice if you are subtly trying to convince yourself of something, giving you the space to decide if it's what you truly want. On the other side of the coin, if you are looking to persuade others, subtly nodding while you're talking increases the likelihood of them agreeing with you.

10. **Be kind.** Kindness is one of the simplest ways to pull yourself out of a funk. By acting kind toward someone, you get out of your own head. The studies on kindness show that it is a powerhouse of positivity.[81] Through a process known as *elevation*, when we do something kind for someone else, it not only makes us and them feel better, it also has the power to make anyone who witnesses it feel good as well. Acting kind changes how we feel about ourselves and how others respond to us.

This chapter covered many topics central to having high hope. We began by looking at the biochemistry of the different emotions.

We learned that by choosing to engage in small actions, stimulating this bit of positivity begins an upward cycle. Taking control of our situation is the fundamental difference between optimism and pessimism. Changing our style to be permanent, pervasive, and personal shifts us toward optimism, and hope increases when we believe and expect we can influence future outcomes. The exercise on cultivating self-compassion helps us overcome self-criticism, the deep inner expression of pessimism, and introduced you to embodied cognition—a way of changing your thinking through action.

In the next chapter, we'll explore how research has identified hope as a character strength, essential to our ability to transcend difficulty.

CHAPTER 5

Focusing on Strengths

"Circumstance does not make me, it reveals me."

—*William James*

Darlene came to my office in her wheelchair. She was permanently disabled and was very proud of her capacity for mobility. Over the years she'd become quite agile. She was gratified by her self-sufficiency, independence, and vitality. It had become a source of her pride and well-being.

One day I heard an altercation take place as she was coming into my office. Anne, the mailwoman, saw Darlene and, without asking her, dropped her mailbag and began pushing Darlene up the slight incline toward my door. Darlene said "I'm okay" several times, then said she'd prefer to do it herself. Anne insisted Darlene needed help and this was where the trouble began. Darlene locked the brakes on her chair and then spoke.

"You helping me isn't what I want," she said, very directly. "I appreciate that you want to be kind—but that's what *you* want. *I* want to do this independently."

Anne was taken aback.

"You helping me when I don't want help is an intrusion," Darlene continued. "If you really want to help someone, ask them first. They'll let you know."

Anne explained that she was only trying to help. Darlene explained that they had different definitions of what was helpful. Anne apologized, and Darlene found her own way into my office.

As it turned out, their schedules often overlapped, and they began seeing one another regularly. They developed a very respectful attitude toward each other, which included Anne asking if she could hold the door for Darlene on occasion, and Darlene either permitting it or Anne respecting Darlene's need to do it on her own.

This encounter informs how a character strength can be overused—and then corrected. One of Anne's obvious strengths was kindness. Her spontaneous effort to help Darlene was authentic. She saw someone she perceived as being in need and went into action. The problem was, her kindness was not calibrated to the situation. Darlene didn't need or want it.

The overuse or underuse of a strength can create interpersonal problems and hitches in well-being. Only when it's used in the right amount for the right circumstance does it have optimal value. By receiving feedback from Darlene, Anne showed her humility and her willingness to improve the relationship. By speaking up about her needs, Darlene displayed her bravery, persistence, and integrity. She was then able to forgive Anne—allowing the relationship to move forward.

Plug into Your Innate Potential

Character strengths—including hope—are power sources that are free, available on demand, universal, creative, and innate. They are within us always, yet are often dormant and waiting to be turned on.

As you will soon learn, there are a total of twenty-four of them—each with unique qualities. They are what allows you to face the next day or hour or moment, even when you wish you didn't have to.

Our character strengths are an essential part of being human and the core of our capacity to survive and thrive. This is why they are essential to identify and cultivate. Without using them, we wither; with them, we have the potential to flourish. The important thing to know is that these strengths are there, waiting for something to help boost them and make them more accessible to us. This has been powerfully demonstrated during misfortunes such as earthquakes, hurricanes, mine collapses, or plane crashes.

Consider what happened when a chartered flight carrying a rugby team traveling from Uruguay to Chile crashed in the Andes in 1972.[82] Of the forty-five people on board, twenty-eight survived the crash. After ten days, rescue efforts were called off. In the bitter cold, high altitude, and icy snow of the Andes, the survivors were without food, warmth, or shelter. They heard the news of the abandoned rescue efforts on a transistor radio. By every measure and assessment of their condition, their situation was hopeless.

Ten weeks later—after seventy-two soul-shattering days on the mountain—sixteen men were rescued. In one of the most dramatic stories of human resilience, these men instinctively used their collective, creative intelligence to survive. Their story made headlines around the world, because it had a lot to teach us about the capacity of the human spirit.

What is informative about their adversity is that their rescue was not about passively maintaining themselves and waiting for something to happen. They didn't just sit in the dark, frozen fuselage and wait. They were saved by their resilience and character.

The characteristics displayed by this group highlight both the survival instinct and the potential built into each of us. It gets activated personally and collectively, which means it's part of our DNA:

we are wired to survive. But we are also wired to thrive. Just like wires or circuits that carry electricity, our DNA wiring transports a form of energy. This energy pulses through the fiber of our being and ignites our essence, pushing us toward survival in creative ways.

Just as electricity is available by plugging into an outlet or connecting to a battery, this power in us is readily accessible, to be used in specific applications. Just as electricity can turn on a light, a toaster, a TV, or a computer, a switch can flip inside us and turn on a deep reservoir of strength. Despite impossible odds and persistent failures, it seems one factor alone made the difference for the plane crash survivors: the *belief* it was possible. As Henry Ford said: "Whether you think you can or think you can't—you're right."

The rugby team demonstrated how essential character strengths like hope and perseverance are available during a disaster—as if the survivors turned on the hope switch. Right now, the same potential is poised inside each of us. Our character strengths are there for us, waiting to be called upon. The question is, how we can access them when we're *not* in a crisis?

Character Strengths Are Your Hidden Superpowers

Traditionally, psychology focused on intelligence and skill as the measures of success. High IQ and high skill level were thought to be the best forecasts of achievement. As it turns out, how well we use our character predicts accomplishment in life about twice as well.

Think of the salesperson who is persistent and uses their social intelligence doing better than the one who knows more about the product. Or the teacher of the year who has humor and zest but whose colleagues graduated with higher GPAs. It's true even of those we think of as being born with a gift. The comedian Steve Martin said of his own career: "Thankfully, persistence is a great substitute for talent."

In the last fifteen years, a developing understanding and use of virtues and character strengths have profoundly influenced the fields of education, business, therapy, coaching, and even government and the military. Character strengths have become the flagship of positive psychology—influencing almost every area of human functioning. Ongoing research has demonstrated that these strengths are what we need not just to survive, but to flourish. They represent an enormous potential inside us.

But what sets them in motion? Do we need a catastrophe to awaken them? Or are they already planted inside us and we just need to nurture them?

At the University of Pennsylvania, the Penn Resilience Program (PRP) has worked with more than 150,000 primary and secondary school children to help develop their resilience and character strengths.[83] They focus on helping students increase self-awareness, self-regulation, mental agility, connection, and optimism, while teaching them what their top character strengths are and how to use them. Their findings show that the students transform when they learn these skills. In addition to reducing conduct disorders, and combating depression, anxiety, and hopelessness, they also improve their mental health, well-being, and life satisfaction. The PRP findings are so powerful, they eventually became the foundation of a program for the world's largest consumer of positive psychology: the US Army.

Beginning in 2009, the US Army has worked with the Positive Psychology Center at the University of Pennsylvania to develop a program for the Army known as Master Resilience Training (MRT).[84] This train-the-trainer program has prepared more than 55,000 soldiers, through the Army's Comprehensive Soldier and Family Fitness program. With more than 1.1 million soldiers who will be educated, it is the world's largest psychology study. Of those who have taken the MRT course, 90 percent have found it helpful or very helpful.

The goal of MRT is to reduce and prevent the adverse psychological consequences of combat for our soldiers and veterans. The original program at the PRP was created to help deal with depression, and the MRT has added to this a focus on the prevention of PTSD and enhancing well-being. Learning how to manage negative thinking and developing one's character are at the very core of this program—just as they are at the heart of what you are learning in this book. Dealing with depression is its own type of combat, and many of the principles that have helped these soldiers are being offered in a modified way here. In the next chapter, we will focus on mental agility and dealing with thinking traps, a component of MRT that participants found particularly useful.

A Handbook to Assess What's Good in Us

Your depression wasn't always with you. There were other, better moments in your life, perhaps really terrific moments—and now they are gone. A loss is often what triggers a depression, or the anxiety that leads to depression. To understand what happens when we feel helpless after a loss, we must first understand what happens when we are fulfilled.

Instead of understanding depression as a chemical imbalance we have to overcome, or a mood disorder we have to be in charge of, what if it were just the result of us not being able to use our strengths? What if it were just us feeling blocked from being who we truly are?

Character Strengths and Virtues: A Handbook and Classification, by Chris Peterson and Martin E.P. Seligman,[85] was designed to offer a compendium of what is right and virtuous in human beings. It was created in direct contrast to the *Diagnostic and Statistical Manual,*[86] a guide for mental health practitioners, used for labeling and diagnosing mental problems—in essence, offering a list of what could be wrong with someone. This work began the revolution in character strengths.

To date, there are over eight million people in nearly two hundred countries who have taken an online character strength survey that is rapidly becoming the go-to vehicle for personal and organizational development. What makes the tool so valuable is that it was developed based on virtues and character traits valued around the world and across all known cultures. A summary description from the VIA Institute on Character website[87] indicates that "Most personality tests focus on negative and neutral traits, but the VIA Survey focuses on your best qualities."

Exploration: Identify Your Character Strengths

I encourage you to take this free test; just do an online search for "VIA character strength survey." You will become part of the database that is helping to change how we approach well-being. Please do this now before reading further, as it will help you understand and use the material in the coming chapters. In your journal, list your top five strengths, in order, along with an example of the last time you used each one.

We all can distinguish warm from cool, bright from dark, happy from sad. These contrasts are important to understand if we want to move between them. We need to know what makes us warm, bright, and happy so we can seek, or create, those conditions when we need them. Character strengths work best when they are in tune with the situation. To use strengths optimally, you must adjust them to the circumstance.

Exploration: Your Strengths in Action

Let's take a look at a time in your life when your depression was absent, or at least less prevalent than it may be now. This was likely a time when your character strengths operated optimally in your life. You'll need your journal for this.

Step 1: Think of a time when everything was going about as well as it could be. This peak period may have lasted a short time, or perhaps even for an entire stage of your life. It's likely to stand out as a time when everything that happened produced a sense of alignment, or what might be called "flow." Your life during this time seemed to be in sync with the universe. You felt good, and there was "effortless effort"—or what is called *wu wei* in Taoism—when you naturally did what you were doing with barely any effort. Remember as many of the details of the experience as you can.

It may be hard to think of these times if you are in a bit of a funk right now, but learning about it will shine an important light on how our well-being operates. Hold this memory in your mind as you write down the details.

Step 2: Look at the following list of character strengths and virtues. You will see the six virtues in bold, and then the character strengths associated with them. As you recall this peak experience, write in your journal the top five or six strengths you were using at that time.

1. *Wisdom and Knowledge:* Creativity or innovation, curiosity, open-mindedness, love of learning, perspective

2. *Courage:* Bravery, persistence, integrity, vitality, zest

3. *Humanity:* Love, kindness, social intelligence

4. *Justice:* Citizenship, fairness, leadership

5. *Temperance:* Forgiveness and mercy, humility, prudence, self-control

6. *Transcendence:* Appreciation of beauty and excellence, gratitude, hope, humor, spirituality[88]

Step 3: Consider these strengths. In writing, reflect on how using a combination of your signature strengths led to your peak experience or powerful positive event. It may have seemed like everything came together via circumstances from the outside, but look at it with this new lens. It is more likely that the positive feelings and experiences you had resulted from using the strengths within you.

Research shows that people who regularly use their top strengths tend to go into flow and as a result report higher levels of well-being, health, and achievement, and fewer psychological issues. You've just identified a list of your strengths—likely several of your top ones—that when used in combination created a peak experience for you. Can you see how using your character strengths is a portal to a better life?

Using our signature character strengths, the top five or so that define the essence of who we are, has been linked to a great many components of well-being. In fact, people who learn what their strengths are and how to use them daily are three times more likely to be having an excellent quality of life and six times more likely to be engaged at work.[89] If you've been feeling depressed or not engaged with life, learning about and using your character strengths may be one of the most direct and sustainable ways to change for the better. Recent research indicates that it's when our strengths are absent that we suffer the most.[90] Imagine not being able to use them.

Exploration: Devoid of Character Strengths

To experience how this works, let's imaginatively take something away that has been working in your life. Don't worry, the good stuff will be immediately returned to you, but first, let me introduce you to an evil wizard.

Step 1: Look at the list of character strengths you were using when you had your peak experience. Try to recall what it felt like to be operating on all cylinders.

Step 2: Now imagine that I have become an evil wizard with the power to take away those strengths: perhaps your love, or courage, or kindness, or creativity. Whatever strengths you were using during the peak experience, they are now utterly unavailable to you. Imagine that I could keep you from using any of those peak strengths for an entire month. List in your journal the feelings that result. Make the list as long as you can.

In workshops, I ask people to shout out words that describe what they would feel without the strengths that brought them their optimal experience. Some words they often yell out are: *lost, empty, helpless, drained, angry, sad, hopeless, worthless, vacant, dead, unhappy, worried, miserable, dull,* and *isolated.* But the one word almost everyone blurts out instantly is *depressed.* Was it on your list?

When we can't use our strengths optimally, we become distraught. It is almost that simple. There is new research that says being unable to use our top strengths may be very detrimental to our well-being and mental health; we'll delve into this soon. Could this be the source of depression? William James, the "father of American psychology," thought so when he declared "If any organism fails to fulfill its potentialities, it becomes sick."

The last exercise was a *positive subtraction,* in which we took away something, to explore what our lives would be like without it. This way, we can appreciate what life is like with it. Think back to how you met your best friend, lover, or spouse and imagine if those circumstances hadn't happened. What would your life be like if you hadn't met? Positive subtraction is an immediate way to have gratitude for what and whom you have in your life.

It Is Possible to Underuse or Overuse Character Strengths

There is another side to character strengths that is important, and perhaps vital, to their understanding and use. Character strengths must be used in the right amount, with the proper sense of balance and calibration. If a violin string is too taut or too loose, we will be out of tune with what is needed for harmony. Too much or too little use of strengths tends to produce less than optimal results.

Take kindness as an example. If we are kind, this is typically a good thing. Helping someone when they are struggling to open a door or carry a package would be hard to see as wrong or bad. But as we saw in the story about Darlene, helping someone when they do not need or want it can be intrusive. The character strength of the mailwoman, Anne—her kindness—had become intrusive because she was overusing it. When it was used in a more calibrated way, it was like the violin string had been appropriately tuned, and harmony prevailed.

A groundbreaking study[91] showed that character strengths' underuse and overuse were related to negative outcomes, while optimal use was related to positive outcomes. More specifically, the overuse of social intelligence and humility, and the underuse of zest, humor, self-regulation, and social intelligence were associated with social anxiety, which is often a precursor for depression. This research gives some insight into how deciding to focus on strengths gives us more control over our depression and well-being than we might have thought we had. By identifying our strengths and using them in a calibrated and optimal way, we are simultaneously enhancing our positivity while avoiding an undesirable experience. It's a happy balance we're after. What I like most about this new approach to mental health is that it isn't just descriptive—it is *prescriptive,* and adjustments can be made accordingly.

Do you have a tendency to overuse a character strength? Do you underuse a strength? If we don't use our strengths in the right way, we'll run into problems. Read through the list of strengths below[92] and see if any of these are out of tune in one way or another. This will give you a road map to help you navigate the optimal use of your strengths.

Strengths	Underuse	Overuse
Creativity	Conformity	Eccentricity
Curiosity	Disinterest	Nosiness
Judgment	Unreflectiveness	Cynicism
Love of Learning	Complacency	Know-It-All-Ism
Perspective	Shallowness	Overbearingness
Bravery	Cowardice	Foolhardiness
Perseverance	Fragility	Obsessiveness
Honesty	Phoniness	Righteousness
Zest	Laziness	Hyperactivity
Love	Emotional Isolation	Emotional Promiscuity
Kindness	Indifference	Intrusiveness
Social Intelligence	Cluelessness	Overanalysis
Teamwork	Selfishness	Dependency
Fairness	Partisanship	Detachment
Leadership	Compliancy	Despotism
Forgiveness	Mercilessness	Permissiveness
Humility	Delusions of Grandeur	Self-Deprecation
Prudence	Sensation-Seeking	Stuffiness
Self-Regulation	Self-Indulgence	Inhibition
Appreciation of Beauty/ Excellence	Obliviousness	Perfectionism
Gratitude	Individualism	Ingratiation
Hope	Negativism	Pollyana-ism
Humor	Over Seriousness	Giddiness
Spirituality	Anomie	Fanaticism

Exploration: Imagine New Ways to Be

Over the next twenty-four hours, think about using one of your top strengths in new and different ways. Be mindful of the "golden mean"—the happy balance of using the strength in just the right way—to adjust it to the situation. Over the next month, use one strength a day in this way so you can learn about each one and its optimal uses. It's best to keep a daily record of your use of the strength and whether it felt like it was in the golden-mean zone. Were you in harmony with your use of the strength in the environment you were in?

Remember, it's how we think about the future that's most important in stimulating hope. Thinking about how you'll use your strengths differently is a way of cultivating your growth. If you find that your strengths are not calibrated optimally, try balancing them to get you functioning at your best.

The Gift of Applying Your Strengths in Ongoing Ways

Up until now, you've been building skills to maximize your ability to alleviate depression and enhance your well-being. But the real issue with depression isn't getting out of it—it's staying out. What I've learned is that relapse prevention requires different skills. This is why our focus has been on learned hopefulness, where we are untangling the habits of thought that keep us stuck and showing the power of optimally using your character strengths. Finding new ways to use your strengths prevents you from getting depressed in the first place, by giving you hope for more control in your life.

Using character strengths helps in relapse prevention by directly bolstering resilience skills and stimulating elements of hope. As you lift yourself out of a minor funk, thinking about how you can use your top strengths is the vehicle for keeping you out—which keeps you moving forward rather than staying stuck. The best way to prevent relapsing into a depression might be best summarized by Bruce Springsteen in his book *Born to Run,*[93] "All you need to do, is risk being your true self."

CHAPTER 6

Creating Challenging Goals

"The greatest trap in our life is not success, popularity, or power,
but self-rejection."

—Henri Nouwen

Amy was quite possibly the most depressed person I've ever worked
with. With Amy, nothing helped. The endless list of medicines her
psychiatrist prescribed, my suggestions about getting herself motivated, and my encouragement for her to get involved in, well, anything, all failed. Amy had an excuse for everything.

Our weekly therapy sessions were the only time she left her house.
She had her groceries delivered, had stopped responding to invites
from her friends, and was sleeping most of the day. But she never
missed a therapy session. She'd show up on time, explain why she
couldn't change, and then make another appointment.

Then one day Amy was late for our appointment, for the first
time. She was apologetic and said she had to stop at a convenience
store to pick up paper plates and it took longer than she expected. I
was beside myself with joy, thinking she was hosting guests. But it
turned out that she had long ago run out of clean dishes and had been
eating off paper plates.

"Have you tried washing the dishes?"

She shook her head. "Too much work. I don't have any energy for that, and what's the difference? No one is coming over to see me anyway. I don't care what the house looks like."

"Washing dishes might give you some control over your living space, and that might make you feel better."

She resisted my suggestion until I got her to agree to wash just *one* dish over the week between our sessions. She left my office reluctantly agreeing to wash one dish. Then that night, she called me. It was the most animated I'd heard her.

"You were right! I washed one and set it on a clean space on the kitchen counter, and it felt great. So weird. That one plate made me, somehow, feel better. I decided to wash another, and seeing the two of them piled on top of each other made me feel like I could do something. I couldn't believe it. I washed a few more, and every time I did another, it gave me a little boost. I'd stack them, put them away, and each time I did another batch, there was this feeling like, I don't know, like my life was going to be okay. It makes me want to clean the whole house."

This was a turning point for Amy, and she finished our therapy together having made positive and sustainable changes, with plans for the future. At our last session, she gave me the same unopened package of paper plates, which she had kept on her counter as a reminder of what worked for her.

Amy's story demonstrates how setting small goals can have a significant impact on how we generate positive emotions and shift our expectations. Getting control of our life is part of recovering from depression. When we are depressed, a certain insecurity invades our thoughts and actions. We lose confidence, capability, and energy. We lose what mattered to us, begin to isolate, and often feel adrift. Our goals fall apart. Then we stop generating meaningful goals because they seem useless in light of our assessment of the future. Has this happened to you?

I've been encouraging you to challenge the decisions behind your beliefs, and to do everything you can to slow down, stop, and reverse your negative thinking. As you've learned, beliefs come from decisions, which generate thoughts to assess the future. When beliefs produce negative thoughts, they keep you stuck in your depression, because your assessment of the future is bleak.

If you've been following along, doing work in your journal, and applying the tools, you are likely making progress. Each of these decisions, beliefs, expectations, and methods has been designed to free you from thinking about your past in a certain way, to see the potential in each moment, and to improve your expectations of the future. This chapter will help you learn how to use goals to grow hope while uncovering limiting beliefs—the thinking traps that stifle them.

Your Goals Need to Be Supported by Others

When we change our perspective for the better, we also need other people to help us maintain our drive. The perspective other people offer us goes a long way, as researcher Kaye A. Herth[94] has shown in her work, which has had a tremendous influence on nursing, medicine, and health psychology. Hundreds of studies support what I am about to share about how people strive toward future goals.

Setting goals keeps us on track and moves us toward productivity. Remember Suzanne, my cancer patient who recalibrated her goals to activate her sense of agency? She learned how to activate hope by finding the right combination of motivation and means. Suzanne was also successful because she turned to other people to support her goals. Our feelings of belonging, of social and spiritual support, sustain hopeful feelings and keep us on track to meeting our goals.

Studies show that social support helps through amplification. Whatever we do to improve our well-being, or to pull us out of a depression, gets magnified when we add social support to the mix. It is like Miracle Grow for our lives. When we feel the support of others, our chance for success improves dramatically. In studies with middle school students, teenagers, and college students, social support amplified how effectively they achieved their goals. They all did better with peer support.

It also works for depression. After a major study out of Oxford[95] of thirty thousand people showed conclusively that mindfulness meditation was as effective as antidepressants, a separate study compared the effects of mindfulness on cancer recovery, with and without social support. The results showed that coping with stress and improved mood, using the mindfulness intervention, was enhanced for those receiving support. Still other studies have demonstrated that the impact of positive events in daily life for people with symptoms of depression are enhanced when they have social support for their goals.[96] In other words, every effort you make toward changing your mood is intensified when you let others help. Social support will not only buffer you against depression—it will also help you achieve your goals.

Why is being with others who support us so powerful? It's because it is a direct connection. Social isolation is often at the core of any depression and can be a major factor in keeping you stuck. A feeling of loneliness often reflects the gap between what we want in relationships and what we have, between what we desire and our relationships as they actually are. You can have many connections in your life—with a spouse and coworkers, say—yet internal conflict, doubt, and hesitation can leave you feeling emotionally lonely. If this is true for you, you may feel lonely even when others are around. This type of loneliness has been linked to persistent problems with the immune system, stress responses, heart health, and diseases. It chronically robs your energy and reinforces your negative thinking. When you reach out for social support, as you'll gather ways to do in Chapter 8, even if it feels difficult, this one effort can help you change very quickly for the better.

I want to be careful to separate out healthy alone time versus social isolation. Some instances in life (like writing a book) require focused thought and less social contact. Time for reflection, meditation, and concentrated effort on a project can be exceptionally helpful in improving our well-being. This is different from social isolation and the emotional loneliness we've been discussing.

While the losses in our lives can create the beginning of depression, adding others into our lives can be the greatest source of what makes us well.

Be SMART About Simple Goals

By taking my suggestion, and washing one dish rather than trying to change everything all at once, Amy unlocked her journey toward hopefulness, generating an upward spiral of energy. The positive feelings continued to expand, allowing her to set and achieve larger goals. She didn't know it at the time, but she was engaging in one of the most effective techniques for pulling herself out of a slump: she started small, built on that, made her success visible, and shared her progress with a supportive person. These are the essential features of successful goal achievement that helps untangle you from the clutches of depression.

One of the most effective forms of goal-setting is what's known as SMART goals. This acronym stands for Specific, Measurable, Actionable, Realistic, Timely.[97] Each plays an important role in making goals happen. Let's walk through them.

- In identifying a **S**pecific goal, you take a generalized goal like "I want to lose some weight" and make it specific: "I want to lose ten pounds."

- This also makes it meaningfully **M**easurable. You can weigh yourself when you begin, and as you go along.

- Losing ten pounds and measuring your progress means there is something **A**ctionable happening. You choose vegetables rather than fries with your sandwich, or skip dessert after dinner.

- To make it **R**ealistic, you give yourself six months, not six days.

- Finally, this type of goal must be **T**imely. You wouldn't give yourself ten years to lose the ten pounds—you'll want the timeline to engage you in the process.

Imagine if your goal was: "I want to lose some weight over the next ten years, without measuring myself." Compare this to: "I want to lose ten pounds in the next six months, measuring my progress every other week." Setting a SMART goal has everything to do with achieving it.

In the course of this chapter, you'll be setting some goals for yourself. The key will be to pick small goals that will give you success and build toward larger ones. Start small and build on it. To make the success visible, you might want to use a calendar or app that lets you take note of your progress. By starting with a tiny goal, you'll build on the confidence that results from each goal met. This is an end unto itself, and the confidence alone will inspire you to continue.

Remember, social support helps because it amplifies and augments the interventions in two ways. First, it gives you a sense of accountability. Second, the accountability increases commitment. Social support also helps to keep us from doing damage to ourselves, or from falling into thinking traps.

Thinking Traps That Keep Us from Our Goals

I realize that looking at the ways in which your thoughts may be sabotaging you isn't easy, but as John Spence, business thought leader, has said: "You cannot change what you refuse to confront." Remember in Chapter 1, I asked you to write down where you are stuck and what negative thoughts repeat themselves? I mentioned that these are the thoughts that hold you back the most, and identifying them is the first step in challenging their power over you.

You've identified them, and we are now going to face them directly. First, look at your list. Repetitive thoughts are important because they are like a front-wheel-drive car. They can turn the car in one direction or the other. Repetitive negative thoughts turn the wheels hard left and keep us going in circles. Check out the list below. Have you had any of these thoughts? If you have, chances are you've been caught in a thinking trap.

Thinking traps are habits of thought that cause a pattern of reactions to unfold within us. They interrupt the intake of information about a situation, and therefore color the situation according to our habit of mind. They are very common, and learning to spot them and challenge them is an effective way to reduce suffering, change perspective, and increase joy. While there are many versions of thinking traps, here are some you might recognize in yourself and others. You may have even written some of these down yourself during the exercise in Chapter 1.

I'm not good enough.

I know I'll mess up.

I'll never be able to manage my anxiety.

I can't do it.

I'm not lucky.

I should just give up.

Anything less than perfect is a failure.

I messed up—now everything is ruined.

I'll never become what I want to be.

I'm not strong enough.

I should be better than I am.

I can't do anything about it.

Others think I'm stupid.

She doesn't like me.

Nobody cares.

Nobody loves me.

I always make mistakes.

I'm stupid.

I'm a loser.

I'll faint.

I'll go crazy.

I'll freak out and no one will help.

I'll make a fool of myself and be embarrassed.

I can't win.

It's too late.

I'm not smart enough.

I'm a failure.

No matter what I do, things won't change.

What's wrong with me?

I may as well die.

I can't control my feelings.

I should never make mistakes.

When one of these thoughts—or several of them—repeats in your mind, it's being generated from an underlying belief system. The repetition is a trap.[98] This is one way to notice that your thoughts have entered into a downward spiral: the repetition is a signal that your thinking has become unbalanced. Thinking traps come in all different sizes and shapes, but they all have one thing in common—repetition.

A one-off thought won't do too much damage, and it may hardly be noticed. But a constant barrage creates a problem. Beliefs are repetitive habits of thought. Thinking traps are repetitive *negative* beliefs that influence your assessment of the future. Repeating negative beliefs will limit you. Noticing the pattern to your thought process is where the change begins. If you become aware that there's a pattern, you're more likely to be able to change it for the better. Here are some common thinking traps.[99] Let's see if any of them apply to you and what you can do about it.

All-or-nothing thinking (or *black-and-white thinking*) happens when only extremely good or bad options seem possible. The idea of a "gray" or "beige" option isn't happening—nothing in between is considered. Things are either good or bad, a success or a failure, right or wrong. For example, cheating once on your diet does not mean you have failed completely. You had a small setback, and all you need to do to correct it is get back on your diet tomorrow. Here are some examples of black-and-white thinking: *Anything less than perfect is a failure.* Or, *I had a piece of candy. Now my diet is ruined!*

Jumping to conclusions is when you make an assumption without enough information. For example, Amy assumed being divorced would forever leave her single. These types of assumptions need to be challenged with facts, such as the fact that most people find love again after a divorce. Thinking traps are clever, and they pull in our behavior to support the illusion. Since Amy never went anywhere she might meet someone, her thinking trap dominated because she wasn't engaging in behavior that could challenge it. If you call your boyfriend and he doesn't answer when you think he should, a jumping-to-conclusions trap would start you thinking: *He's having an affair, he's supposed to be home right now, and he's not answering—I bet he's with someone else.* You've come to a conclusion that doesn't allow for other information, like him being caught in traffic, or taking a shower.

Mind-reading is when you believe you know what others are thinking or assume others know what you're thinking. Here are some examples of mind-reading: *Nobody loves me. People think I'm stupid. She doesn't like me. Nobody cares.*

Overgeneralizing happens when we make sweeping judgments about ourselves (or others) based on minimal experience: *Nobody cares. Nobody loves me. I'm a failure. I'll never win. I'm a loser. I'm not smart enough.* They take one bad experience and turn it into something that distorts our view. Words like "always" and "never" are often used in this type of trap: *I'll never be able to manage my anxiety. I always make mistakes.* When Amy's one friend didn't call her, she assumed none of her friends cared about her anymore. Mind-reading got piled on top of overgeneralizing—sometimes thinking traps work together to hold us back.

Negative brain-filtering is the ultimate form of pessimism. Everything is filtered through a negative lens. Only the negatives are noticed. You give a terrific presentation; then you notice one person out of the group looks bored and think everyone hated it. This is an ultimate form of pessimism because no matter what happens that's good, you're going to focus on what went wrong, what wasn't working, or what was a disappointment. It's common for thinking traps to work together. You might filter the negative view of how people responded to your presentation and then overgeneralize: *I'm not good at public speaking.*

Personalizing or *externalizing* occurs when everything is either your fault or someone else's. By personalizing, you take too much responsibility for the situation, and by externalizing you make things someone else's fault and not yours. *No matter what I do, things won't change. What's wrong with me? They never get it right.*

Overestimating or *catastrophizing* exaggerates the likelihood something bad will happen. We imagine the worst and/or believe we won't be able to cope with the outcome. The truth is that the worst very rarely happens, and if it does we usually find a way to cope. Catastrophizing saps us of our life force and energy: *I'll freak out. No one will help me if I screw up. I'll make a fool of myself and will be too embarrassed.* These are typical ways we convince ourselves of how bad things are going to be.

Fortune-telling is the mantra of those who believe they can see the future and it isn't bright: *I'll faint. I'll go crazy. I'm not strong enough. I can't win. I'll never become what I want to be. I'm not strong enough. I can't do it.* The truth is, these thoughts actually do make success less possible, because they limit our effort and our belief in possibility.

"Should" statements. The famous psychologist Albert Ellis said people "should" on themselves all the time and they are "must-er-baters." Constantly telling yourself how you should or must behave is a surefire way to keep yourself feeling anxious and disappointed in yourself and others. These are easy to identify because they have the terms right in them: *I should never feel worried. I must control my feelings. I should never make mistakes.*

Exploration: Identify Your Thinking Traps

In your journal, look at that original list of negative thoughts that get you stuck and identify the thinking trap they each might represent. Likely, not every one of your thoughts will fit neatly into one of the classifications—but see which ones do. It's less important that you identify the *type* of trap and more important to understand that the repetitive negative thought *is* a trap. Look for the thoughts that routinely crowd your mind.

At this point in your self-reflection and exploration exercises, you should be able to see how repetitive thoughts create beliefs influencing your future. Reflect on this in your journal. What do these negative thoughts keep you from? What do they predict? Would you want to change them if you could?

Dismantling Your Traps to Reenvision the Future

Hope can be cultivated in many ways when it comes to thinking traps and depression. You can identify and then build on your character strengths, challenge your thinking directly, or use small goals to pull you out of the ditch of depression. Micro-goals give immediate support to our potential and have the power to restore the energy we need to recalibrate our expectations. *Our beliefs can change our actions, and our actions can change our beliefs.*

To break a thinking trap, you have to dispute the assumption being made. Most resilience programs will begin with you learning about your repetitive negative thoughts, and then help you develop strategies for challenging your assumptions. The key to dismantling a thinking trap is to realize that a decision is being made about how to behave in the future. Not to confront and object to these decisions is choosing to keep them the same. *Not choosing to make things better is a decision to remain in pain.*

Exploration: Challenge Traps with Possibility

Now that you have identified the repetitive negative thought (sometimes referred to as ANT, for Automatic Negative Thought[100]) you are having, and which type of trap it is, challenge the assumption behind it. Look for evidence to the contrary. You can weaken thinking traps by finding ways to challenge each thought with other possibilities. Did you jump to a conclusion too quickly because you didn't consider another likelihood? Is your black-and-white thinking taking everything into account? Probably not. What did you overlook? Instead of mind-reading, could you ask for information from others or speak up to check out your assumptions? This type of contrary evidence requires you to reflect on your ANTs and test the validity of these beliefs. Review your thinking traps and note the evidence to the contrary.

In each challenge, you are broadening your search by looking for more information, taking a different perspective, or questioning whether a salient piece of information was overlooked.

If you need evidence to the contrary, the clearest way to demonstrate that a thinking trap is not true is to use goals (often micro-goals) to *create* evidence to the contrary. Take one of the most common negative beliefs, *I can't do it,* which is a type of fortune-telling that becomes a self-fulfilling prophecy. A micro-goal challenging this belief uses action to confront the validity of the belief.

Thinking traps limit our beliefs, and consequently limit hope for achieving our goals. My friend Cathi was always interested in writing a book and telling her story. But whenever I encouraged her to do it, she said she couldn't. She didn't have the talent, the stamina, the discipline, and on and on. I kept suggesting she should try—she kept telling me she couldn't. Finally, I encouraged her to simply write the opening sentence to the book. What would that sentence be? How would she begin the book she would write if she could? Nothing else—just the opening sentence. She emailed the sentence to me two days later. It was a real attention-grabber and I told her so. She was very proud of her sentence and I asked her what the first paragraph would be. The paragraph became the first chapter, then a book outline, and although it took several years, Cathi wrote a book proposal that was accepted by an agent and eventually a publisher. Cathi proved to herself that her belief system was wrong by achieving micro-goals that proved the opposite to be true. Her success inspired continual progress, because she was proving her negative belief, her thinking trap, to be wrong.

When the psyche is confronted with conflicting information, it naturally grows. Think of a child who doesn't believe they can ride a bike, but wants to. They don't believe they can until they do. You probably have this memory, whether about learning to ride a bike or something else—that moment of possibility that you can do something because you are doing that very thing, even though you didn't think it was possible. Accomplishing a micro-goal weakens the trap of a negative belief.

Understanding the power that thinking traps have over our behavior, and devising ways to dismantle them, has resulted in the dramatic results of the large-scale programs you learned about in Chapter 5. By helping students of various ages not only learn about their strengths, but also learn strategies to confront different thinking traps, the Penn Resilience Program (PRP)[101] has been effective in reducing depressive symptoms in participants who then showed fewer symptoms for as long as a year after the thinking traps were challenged. These studies were the backbone of the Master Resilience Training used by the US Army—doing exactly the same thing for adults.[102] By combining an understanding of our strengths with strategies and practices to dismantle the negative beliefs behind thinking traps, these programs have been effective in reducing depression without resorting to medicine.

Climbing Out of the Dark Through Calibrated Goals and Micro-Goals

When a goal is too far out of reach, we feel defeated before we begin. Uncertainty must be present for hope to kick in. If you are certain your effort isn't going to work, then why bother? If you're convinced that no matter how much you train, you could never run a marathon, you wouldn't be motivated because of your certainty—it's *never* going to happen. Also, big goals don't pay off the same way small goals do. Every day until you achieve the goal feels like a failure, because it's too far away.

Science has informed us that smaller goals keep us motivated, engaged, and connected to the larger accomplishment we're after. Small goals are the handrails on the steps to success. Modifying the major goal into smaller ones (such as running a 5K, a 10K, and a half-marathon as milestones for a marathon) begins the movement toward the goal, to engage hope. The more calibrated the goal, the more possible it becomes.

The purpose of setting micro-goals is to begin moving toward them. These small goals must have some challenge, some uncertainty for them to get traction. If the goal is too easy to accomplish it won't motivate us. Achieving it begins to shift our thinking about what may be possible, rather than focusing on our certainty about what isn't—opening us up to the possibility of accomplishing larger goals in the future. This effort is where hope is born.

Our goals are shaped by what we believe we need, want, and have a chance of attaining. Creating a goal starts with the belief that it's possible to accomplish it. With Amy, by calibrating her goal to something granular—washing one dish—we increased what was possible by reducing the distance between her beliefs and her effort. Yet goals also challenge your negative beliefs. Once they are set, the uncertainty is in whether you'll follow through. You are moving toward them "as if" they are possible to achieve. Action gets you out of the thinking trap and shifts the belief system. You might have doubts about doing a marathon, but buying a new pair of sneakers, or walking an extra mile a week, are micro-goals that would be in line with a larger one.

Exploration: Choose Goals That Free You from Thinking Traps

What can you do to challenge the thinking traps you've identified? What small action can help defy your negative thoughts? For Cathi it was one sentence; for Amy it was one dish. What will yours be?

In your journal, look at your original list of repetitive thoughts or stuck emotions from Chapter 1. Pick three to work with. This exploration is designed to show you the process. You can always go back and do it again to develop the practice.

Step 1: Write down one of the thinking traps you identified in a previous exercise that you would like to address. Just doing this means you've begun making the necessary changes because you've introduced a bit of uncertainty into your habit of thought. Then identify the goal it is blocking you from accomplishing.

For Amy, not washing the dishes came from her negative repetitive thought: "Why bother?" This was part of her overgeneralizing thinking trap. Since her "all-or-nothing" thinking was confirming nothing would ever change—she overgeneralized to "Why bother?" with anything. The dishes just kept piling up. The goal it was blocking was cleaning up the dishes. Which thinking trap is *your* negative thought tied to, and what goal is it blocking?

Step 2: Look at your goal and think of it in terms of a calibrated, small goal. What is a calibrated goal for you—some portion of the whole goal? If not the whole marathon, what about a half, or a 6K? Write down your calibrated goals.

Step 3: Let's get down to the micro-goal. What is your micro-goal that you'd be willing to experiment with and actually do? It might be as small as Amy's one dish in one week or Cathi's one sentence in two days.

Step 4: Consider how you will seek to support achieving this micro-goal. When will you commit to doing it? Who would you be willing to tell you will do it, and report to once you've done it?

Step 5: Now take this action and do this micro-goal in the time allotted for it. Then tell your designated person. Journal what happened for you in this doing and telling of it. How has it shifted your thinking, your beliefs?

What is the next micro-goal you'll be willing to set in connection to this? Follow the same process. Set the micro-goal, the timeline for it, and whom you'll tell, and then write it all down. Continue with micro-goals until you're ready to set a calibrated goal, timeline, and who you'll tell about it. Micro-goals are a way to jump-start the process. As Marty Seligman says: "set goals...enthusiasm follows."

Reframing the Stress of Making an Effort as Positive

As you act on your micro-goals, you may find yourself resisting the effort it takes. You may find that it's stressful, and you'd rather not bother. In an eight-year study, researchers asked participants a simple question: "Do you believe stress is harmful to your health?" Their findings showed the highest rates of mortality for those who'd experienced a high degree of stress and believed it was harmful to their health. Those with the lowest risk of dying had the same high rates of stress as their counterparts, but didn't believe their stress was harmful.[103] What they believed about the stress markedly changed their ability to survive.

To put this in perspective, this would put the *belief* that stress is bad for you in the top fifteen causes for death—killing more people than HIV, skin cancer, and homicide. It is what we think is happening to us—*our beliefs*—that determine our reaction, and our well-being. This finding points to a key issue for our survival: learning how to modify our beliefs may be one of the healthiest things we can do.

Kelly McGonigal[104] is a health psychologist from Stanford University, and she has been studying the effects of stress on the body and performance. She has found that if we perceive stress as harming our well-being and performance—*it does*. However, if we interpret the signs of stress, like a faster-beating heart and accelerated respiration, as signs of readiness to meet the challenge, it may be beneficial to our body, and performance. In fact, a Harvard research team demonstrated that when participants in a stress-induced situation were told to experience these physiological reactions as positive responses—helpful for preparation—it was found that their blood vessels did not constrict as they did for those who saw their physiological reactions as indicators of stress that was bad for them, even though the actual biological measures are physiologically similar to what our body experiences in times of joy and courage.

This shows that it isn't the event that determines the effect on us. It is the interpretation: the *belief* about the incident.

Learning Has Upward Momentum

Like a child learning to walk, emotional growth is developmentally organized. There are repeated failures, each followed by reflection, correction, and progress. You don't go back to crawling once you've learned to walk, and you don't stay stuck in negative thinking once you've learned how to move past it. As we learn to break the bonds of stuck thinking, we may stumble, but once we master how to think about better things, we are drawn to maintain and continue our progress. Showing ourselves that we can achieve even small goals is a powerful way to change our thinking. If you've ever watched a child's persistence in learning to stand, to walk, and to ride a bike, you've seen that the struggle to make slight improvements fuels the effort to continue. This is why confronting our negative beliefs with small actions that contradict them is so important. Micro-goals create evidence to the contrary about our negative thinking.

The biggest challenge to personal growth is facing ourselves. As each of the interventions has shown, whether it is how we view stress, talk to ourselves, handle fixed mindsets, or deal with thinking traps, each transformation toward better things begins with encountering ourselves. This is the essential ingredient in making change happen. Unless we reflect on our thought process, and experiment with actions to challenge it, change isn't likely. Imagine trying to remove a splinter from your eye without the aid of a mirror. The irritation gets worse until you see where the problem is—then you experiment with ways to remove it.

Micro-goals help us invest in a world that hasn't happened yet, because setting them contradicts our negative beliefs while fueling our sense of accomplishment. Identifying the negative beliefs holding us back and activating a new possibility of what we can control in the future is what initiates hope. These new habits of thought and action that we are cultivating promote ongoing positive expectations of control over the future. Once we've done the hard work of facing ourselves and getting released from our traps, it's like we've finally climbed out of a very deep hole. Now that we've escaped from our self-designed prison—which way do we go? How do we make sure we don't fall in again?

We've gotten used to operating in the dark—now we have to get used to the light. Our purpose before was to get out of the darkness. Now that this has happened, we have to find our way.

CHAPTER 7

Finding Purpose

"Each man must look to himself to teach him the meaning of life.
It is not something discovered: it is something molded."

—*Antoine de Saint-Exupéry*

Jordan started drinking at thirteen, dropped out of high school by sixteen, and before he was twenty, he'd been to jail twice. Early in life, his outlook wasn't good. Jordan wasn't a nice guy as a teenager or young man. He got into endless fights, felt entitled to everything, and stole cars, people's possessions, and others' girlfriends. When he got one of the girls pregnant, he married her in a shotgun wedding demanded by the girl's father. He had two more children with this woman, but was never faithful during the entire five-year marriage. He had a short temper and reported that barely a week went by before he was coming home bleeding from some fight—he lost as many as he won.

His drinking and drugging got worse. He sold drugs to get by at first, and then he walked out on his family to pursue bigger plans as a drug lord. He was a natural. He went from making about a thousand dollars a week to about fifty thousand a month. He flashed his money, his cars, and his clothes. At one point, he was selling everything from stolen cars to women to cocaine. He seemed untouchable—no remorse, no boundaries, and no sign of changing.

Then Jordan was ambushed by two men who beat him with baseball bats, breaking seventeen bones in his body. They weren't there to kill him; they were there to send a message. During the ambush, his home was robbed and a moving truck took off with much of his stuff. His cars were taken, and then his house burned to the ground. Jordan thought he had lost everything.

After nearly six months of hospitalization and twelve operations, he was released, still wearing a cast. He was clean and sober, but had no friends and precious little money. He moved into a boarding room with the little he had. That night, the same men broke down his door and swung their bats again. This time it would be eight months before he'd come home from the hospital.

Jordan was referred to me almost fifteen years after all of this happened. It took that long to accumulate a few years of sobriety. His life was stalled completely. He had trouble holding a job or maintaining a relationship, and his three children, all young women now, wouldn't return his calls. The bats had broken more than his bones— they had broken his identity and his belief in himself. All he could talk about was how stupid he had been and how his life was ruined. While he had some pride over his recovery, he didn't see it helping him beyond stopping things from getting worse. His vision of his future seemed bleak.

In this chapter, I will share more of Jordan's story as we look at what helps us come back from loss—however devastating—to ultimately find the sense of purpose that will drive us into a meaningful future. By finding purpose, you can walk a path that avoids the vortexes of depression. More important, when you hit life's turbulence every now and again, you will be able to navigate it without getting knocked out of commission.

Making the Most of Feeling Pushed and Pulled

While we usually think of getting pushed and pulled in various directions by external forces—like family demands, earning a paycheck, raising children, even politics—we also experience these forces inwardly. Pushing away from one thing and pulling something else toward us are two primary energy sources that reveal our motivations. When we are pushed, we are mostly moving away from something, and when we are pulled, we are being drawn in. We need both push- and pull-forces to get where we want to go—and we can harness them.

Take the first step toward building the motivation you need to explore your purpose. Think of what you want to move away from and imagine what you want to move toward.

Jordan used the push-force to turn away from harmful decisions, negative beliefs, and current inaction. In the process, he applied the skills you have learned in past chapters, like changing your mindset, undoing thinking traps, and setting micro-goals. He then used the pull-force of using his strengths of creativity, appreciation of beauty and excellence, love of learning, and social intelligence. Once he learned to balance these things, he could move toward life with purpose and meaning.

In the same way, you may have used the push-force to get out of your depression funk. Moving away from what's holding you back releases your mind from ruminating and returns you to who you naturally are. You break away from a habit and come back to what is more natural. You were not meant to be stuck in depression, and your strengths offer the pull-force you need to move toward greater hope. So does a sense of purpose.

Feeling the Call, or Pull, of Genuine Purpose

When we feel called to do something, we are pulled toward it. Following this pull-force gives our lives deeper meaning and fortifies us to fulfill that goal. Those who have a calling, something that gives significant meaning to their life, transcend the slings and arrows of failure, disappointment, and setback, because they are being pulled by something greater.[105] This doesn't mean there aren't moments of letdowns and frustration, but it does mean that there is an abundance of high hope that drives their journey.

So let the pull-force influence you. What do you feel drawn to accomplish, create, express, be, do? How do you want to mold your purpose?

Angela Duckworth[106] offers this parable as an aid: "Three brick-layers are asked, 'What are you doing?' The first says, 'I am laying bricks.' The second says, 'I am building a church.' And the third says, 'I am building the house of God.' The first bricklayer has a job. The second has a career. The third has a calling." What is intriguing is that to an outside observer, all three bricklayers are doing the same thing. It is their perspective on what they are doing that makes the difference.

The bricklayer who has a job sees his work as a means to an end. He is more pushed to do it than pulled. Are your life chores, job, or roles like this? Do you feel you have to do them, more out of necessity than out of true passion? Perhaps you are more like the bricklayer who has a career. Are you in your roles because you are good at them and they are part of your identity? While this can be more motivating, it is still derived more from push than pull.

Imagine arriving at your job site every day invigorated and inspired. Imagine feeling that the activity is effortless—even joyful. As Nietzsche said: "He who has a why to live for can bear almost any how." Soon I'll guide you to find those things that call you to do them with a force that can pull you into the future that you long to live.

Small Successes Build Hope

Jordan did a lot of work to reach this point of the journey. At the outset, I asked him to write down three things he was grateful for every day, just as I asked you to do. Little by little, searching for things he could have gratitude for became a habit and the list grew. From simply being grateful for the day, he started to acknowledge the relationships he'd built in AA, felt appreciation for the skills of the doctors who had helped him heal, was thankful to his employer, and on from there.

We then set some micro-goals. Jordan was ashamed that he hadn't finished high school, and the cascade of negative beliefs and thinking traps behind that was extensive. But just as thinking traps like these can work together to keep us down, they can fall like dominoes when one of them topples. As one negative belief changes, it gives us hope that our other thoughts can also be challenged. Jordan chose the two traps that seemed to be his biggest stumbling blocks: *I'm not smart enough* and *No matter what I do, things won't change.*

Just as you did in the previous chapter, we set micro-goals for Jordan, small goals that progressed like this: learn about getting the GED, locate an information session, attend the session, sign up for classes, and, finally, attend the classes.

Your micro-goals can open up possibility too, and your accumulated sense of success can make thinking traps invalid. This allows you to envision more for your life, and to feel a realistic sense of hope that what you want is attainable.

Small Ways to Create Big Possibilities

Micro-goals can be used to pull us out of negative thoughts, beliefs, and behavior. We can learn to make decisions that push away destructive beliefs, untangle us from negativity, and move us toward purpose and meaning. Finding ways to *not* get into a depression rut in the first place is crucial.

What are the early signs of depressive thoughts and actions? Recognizing and catching the first signs of low mood goes a long way toward staying clear of depression. The clinical view is that anxiety often precedes and accompanies depression. Perhaps you've noticed that if you feel anxious for too long, it tends to sour into a depression. This is most often how it goes—some form of anxiety about our situation bubbles up and leads to a depression.

It's hard to think about meaning and purpose in our lives if we are constantly fighting off anxious or depressed feelings. We want to deal with these thoughts early because, as the hope circuit I shared in Chapter 1 predicts, being in a painful condition too long can cause us to feel hopeless, like things will never be any different.

One micro-goal is to interpret certain bodily functions differently. The sooner you can derail a decision to choose a negative interpretation of your physical experience, the easier it is to activate feelings of hope. Oxford's David Clark taught people how to reinterpret their bodily sensations more productively by reframing their anxious fears with such phrases as "exam nerves help focus attention" or "a little extra adrenaline makes for a better interview."[107] He changed how subjects thought about their bodily reactions to fear, and once they did this, they reframed their symptoms into assets—keeping themselves from becoming increasingly worried and panicked. They didn't activate the helpless switch, which led to much better results.

When you train your body to reinterpret anxiety symptoms (restlessness, racing thoughts, trembling) as indications that your body is preparing you for the upcoming task, you move toward challenges with a strong readiness to meet them and succeed. By not letting your belief system interpret your reactions as negative, but rather as preparatory, there's less to hold you back.

I've trained a number of actresses in preparing for auditions in this way. Instead of their bodily reactions being interpreted as worry, they interpret them to mean that they are getting ready to do their best. Inevitably, this way of thinking helps them during their performance. This can work for you too, once you identify what pulls you toward a life of purpose.

Exploration: What Would You Like to Be Remembered for Most?

To find purpose and meaning, it can help to get a better understanding of where we are in our life by looking at it from a different view. You'll need your journal for this exercise.

Step 1: Begin by writing down the three most important things you did in the last twenty-four hours and why you feel they were significant.

Step 2: Then jump into the future and write a realistic autobiography, as brief or as long as you wish. Begin by brainstorming what the title would be. Consider what you'd be most known for. Write down what actions you took to get where you are. Highlight what you've overcome and your personal strengths as you write this biography. Do you have any regrets? Are there any actions you wish you'd taken? What are you most proud of? What was the turning point for you?

Step 3: Now look at the list you made from the last twenty-four hours and compare it to your autobiography. Are they aligned? Are you living your life each day in accord with how you'd like to be remembered? Reflect on this and write down your thoughts about it, especially if you identify some actions that need to change for the story to align with your daily activities.

Research has shown that writing autobiographies helps people more directly realize their potential while amplifying what is important to them in life.[108] Daily journaling helps keep us on track. In fact, there may be more than eighty ways that journaling about your life can have a positive impact while reducing the symptoms of depression.[109] Looking at life through the lens of a biography helps develop a positive expectation of control in the future, and looking back on life forces us to compare where we are with where we want to be—and seek to align them.[110] As we amplify or correct our actions, we gain meaning and purpose as we aspire to what we would like to be remembered for most.

As Jordan's skills of lifting himself out of depression became stronger, his desire to earn his GED grew and pulled him toward it. We role-played what it would feel like for him to receive the diploma and see his name on it. We did this a lot, and in these enactments he cried almost every time. We made a best possible selfie of the diploma that he kept on his cell phone. He could feel the pride, and he could begin to expect that it was possible. Jordan could imagine a future he had more control over, and was releasing himself from his traps. He finally had hope.

On his tenth anniversary of being sober, Jordan's three daughters showed up for the celebration at his group home. They also brought a cake to celebrate something else: he'd just received his GED. His sobriety, following the AA motto of "one day at a time," and getting his GED proved that Jordan's negative beliefs about himself were wrong. He was smart enough, and he had proved to himself that things do change.

Using Action to Influence Feelings

So how can you get there too? We think our thoughts and feelings cause reactions in our body, but it also works the other way around. We can use action to transform our thoughts through "acting as if," a.k.a. "fake it till you make it." You can act in ways that inspire you to feel good.

I call this the acting cure.[111] It's a collection of techniques that transform feelings through psychodrama, drama therapy, and role-playing, in ways that last and expand beyond the exercise. One reason this happens is that role-playing methods reach the core of emotions. Most people in depression get stuck not only with repetitive thoughts (replaying words) but with repetitive scenes (replaying hurtful movies in their heads). Using psychodrama and other enactment methods, we deconstruct those scenes and replace them with different ones:

scenes that generate hope. Through this direct engagement with the real feelings and memories you are trying to change, rather than talking *about* an image, a feeling, and what can be done to improve it—we are feeling and changing it simultaneously. In Chapter 4, I introduced *embodied cognition* as a way to work with how thoughts affect our entire being, including our body. Thoughts don't just come from our brain alone—they are influenced, even governed, by our experiences in the physical world.

While other therapies have a similar tactic of reimagining scenes as part of the healing process, the use of action amplifies and accelerates the process—especially if you process nonverbal methods better. They say that "Your issues are in your tissues." Because our feelings develop before our ability to use words, it could take a child three, four, or five years to gather enough vocabulary to describe what they are feeling emotionally and in their body. Often, this leads to the storage of painful memories in the body. Leading trauma researcher Bessel Van der Kolk has advocated for the use of psychodrama, yoga, and other nonverbal methods as more direct ways of unlocking our painful memories.

These methods are powerful. My early work with them demonstrated just how helpful they can be to highly traumatized people and patients that the clinical community regards as incurable. Words just couldn't get to the heart of their issues, as many were psychiatrically and intellectually disabled, with limited use of words. After we rehearsed healthy scenes and acted out dramas of feeling supported, people initially expected to need lifelong hospitalization were able to move out into communities. These methods have become widely used in the field of intellectual disabilities, and I've written extensively about them in peer-reviewed journals. I also detailed the origin of these methods in a memoir, *American Snake Pit: Hope, Grit, and Resilience in the Wake of Willowbrook,*[112] which was America's worst asylum. Psychodrama and role-playing enhance and deepen the ways positive psychology can be used in psychotherapy, education, coaching, and healing. By engaging a method that involves action, like you will do in the exercises for this chapter, you are more able to change.

Act Your Way Out of the Depression Trap

We don't just have thinking traps—we also have *acting traps.* To give you an idea of how acting habits are embedded into your life just outside of your awareness, the next time you shower, deliberately do your routine out of order. If you shampoo first, do that later. If you lather up your body starting with your neck, begin at your toes. If you brush your teeth with your right hand, use your left. Our habit of doing it a certain way comes under inspection only when we change it. We might not even be aware we are in an acting trap until we challenge our actions by doing something deliberately different.

Negative acting traps (or NATs, as I like to call them) are the routines of behavior we slip into that are unhealthy for us. We are usually only marginally aware of these routines, yet they keep us stuck in a pattern of behavior that maintains depression. Often these acting traps work hand in hand with thoughts to keep us stuck. We'll eat dinner in front of the TV rather than take a walk—and then convince ourselves we need to rest. The acting traps are the dark side of the "as if" principle. If we act *as if* we are tired and have no interest, that is exactly what will happen. In this way, we can "fake it 'til we *break* it."

The acting cure uses enactment and role-playing to explore, or transform. It works in a way similar to the adage "move a muscle, change a thought." It helps undo acting traps by using positive enactments to change thought patterns. The words you think and your actions are linked. When your thoughts are stuck, so is your body.

You took part in this with the exercise exploration in Chapter 4 called "Consult Your Kind Self."[113] When you embody an aspect of yourself, you can enhance your experience, get a different perspective, and shift your point of view. This will happen whenever you play a role, because it liberates you from being stuck in how you are and gives you the opportunity to try on other ways of being.

The two upcoming exercises will help you gather small acts that make a big difference in your sense of purpose in life, by relating with past, present, and future. To get ready for these exercises, set up three chairs in a row—front to back—which will indicate your future (front chair), present (middle chair), and past (back chair).

Exploration: The Past You Got Through on Your Way to Now

This exercise will help you identify the actions you have taken in the past to get through hard times. It will also help you remember all the things that can help change any given situation or mindset. You will need your journal for this.

Step 1: Sit in your present (middle) chair and bring your journal with you. Write down at least three good things that are in your life that weren't ten years ago. Think of people, experiences, jobs, possessions, opportunities, and circumstances that are good—and that didn't exist in your life a decade in the past. Make the list as long as you like, but be sure to have at least three.

Step 2: Switch seats and sit in your past (back) chair. Think of three things that were not going well back then—about ten years ago—but have changed for the better somehow. Write down only three things.

Step 3: Turn your present (middle) chair around, sit in it, and face your past. Talk to your past self. Remind yourself how you dealt with these three things that weren't going well.

- What did you do that allowed you to get to the present?

- What new people showed up to help make the change?

- What resources did you draw on?

- What risks did you let yourself to take?

- How did you take control?

- Which of your strengths did you use to get through those times?

- What support, whether social or spiritual, was there for you?

- Who did you rely on for support?

- What micro-goals or big goals helped pull you through?

Answer these questions and write down what present-you has to say to past-you.

Step 4: Look at this list and reflect on the skills you readily activated during your time of need. Highlight or circle them. What do you notice about your answers? Maybe there was one person whose support really helped. Maybe you remembered an unexpected meeting or connection that changed your course for the better. Maybe you let go of things that were no longer true. Write down your reflections and insights.

When we are repeating negative thoughts and ruminating about our misfortunes, it is difficult to recall and reflect on the transformations we've had that were beneficial. Just like doing the shower routine differently, this exercise changes our perspective, and in doing so highlights the way we've been doing things well. Looking at your past through the lens of what worked can support you and highlight what you could also do in the present.

Once you've seen for yourself how things have changed, you have powerful evidence that you can draw on at any time. Anytime you make a decision about how to respond to a situation, feeling, or event, you are choosing between a high-hope response, a thinking trap, an acting trap, or a negative interpretation. In this chapter, I am empowering you to make early adjustments to your thinking so your decisions and actions move you toward hope. Intervening in this way—early on—will give you the greatest amount of control. This is not an effort to avoid pain, but rather a direct attempt to not let it dominate your well-being. Once you've gotten out of a depression hole, this is the skill that will keep you from relapsing.

When all is said and done, role-playing and acting "as if" are rehearsals for life. Jacob Moreno, founder of psychodrama, group therapy, and social network theory, described psychodrama this way and saw the magic of "as if" as a progression where the "if" falls away, leaving only "as."[114]

Jordan's sobriety and GED showed him that he—and life—can indeed change, and this knowledge lit a fire under him. He recalled that, in the fancy home he had back in the day, he had done all the landscaping, including all the stone and patio work with brick and slate. He loved doing it. He found himself pulled again toward its creativity and was soon reading all about it, checking out library books on landscape architecture and stone-wall building. It continued to pull at him, likely because it fed his top three strengths of creativity, love of learning, and appreciation of beauty and excellence.

Soon it was time for him to turn his passion into a business. He borrowed money from a fellow AA member to start it, and just as quickly as he built his drug business, his landscape business grew. Jordan had terrific social intelligence and knew how to approach people and make connections. He formed a limited liability corporation and within a year had ten employees and three trucks. When he paid the loan back, his friend joked that Jordan should name his business "From Drugs to Shrubs."

With purpose instilled in his day-to-day activities, Jordan's life felt fulfilling. He had rebuilt a life after complete devastation—this time in a positive, beneficial direction. And it began with identifying his personal "why."

How do you get your "why"? By what means can you mold purpose into your life, so that you feel pulled by something greater?

Thinking alone won't do this. It is through action that our purpose becomes auspicious. Hope is a verb. Through action, our purpose reveals itself.

Exploration: Moving from the Present into a Future You Are Meant to Live

Arrange your middle chair (present) so it is facing the back of the front chair (your future—the self you are meant to be). The future chair should be facing away from the present. Pick how far in the future you are. Two years? Five? For this exercise, keep it less than ten years. However far in the future it is, move your chair that distance from the present (if it is one year, it would be closer to the present chair than five years would be).

Step 1: Sit in the future chair, and write down, as if you were already living it, what your life is like. Keep in mind our earlier exercise of your biography of how you'd like to be remembered. You can list as many things as you wish about your future self. All that is required is that you believe they might possibly happen in the time you've determined. As an example, you wouldn't create a future self where you've lost a hundred pounds in a month. Some examples are: "I'm sitting on the dock looking at the lake in my new home, enjoying the view and having my morning coffee." "I'm graduating with my degree in accounting and have been offered a good job." "I'm being invited to a party with people I admire."

Step 2: Once you've done this, turn the future chair to face your present and continue sitting in the future chair. Talk to your present self and "remind" the present-you how you got to become the future self you wanted to be.

- What did you do that allowed you to get to the future?

- What did you take control of to make it happen?

- How did you take control?

- What resources did you draw on?

- What risks did you let yourself take?

- Who did you rely on for support?

- How did you modify your goals?

- What successes opened up more doors and possibilities to you?

- What kind of thoughts, people, or actions did you have to replace?

Answer as many of these questions as you can from your future and explain how satisfied you are with your life. Be sure to write down this review as if it were a summary you are giving to "remind" the present. Then, once you've shared how you arrived at who you were meant to be, feel what it's like to have this future.

Step 3: Sit in the future chair "as if" it is happening now. What got you to living a life of purpose? Pay particularly close attention to your body and what it feels like to be doing what you were meant to do. How do you breathe when you are as you were meant to be? How do you sit? Where do you feel the power in your body? What are you most aware of as this sense of purpose and meaning are awakened?

Can you see your future as something that happens because you take control of it? You've made deliberate changes to bring it about, reinterpreted early feelings that could have gone negative, and kept moving toward your pull-force. When we reflect on the core elements, the essence of what it would be like to live a satisfying and fruitful life, we can move toward it through choice and action. Tal Ben-Shahar taught Harvard's largest class in the history of the psychology department, on happiness. He had his students imagine they were in a time machine and could have their 110-year-old self call their today self. This style of future projection has been identified as an antidepressant technique by the psychologist Arnold Lazarus.[115]

With a sense of purpose, you can more easily surf through life, catching a wave to ride. It matters less how long you stay standing, because once you've sampled the exhilaration of balancing yourself within this powerful force, when you fall you just pop back up.

During the second year of Jordan's business, it continued to grow and thrive, and, little by little, Jordan eased into a middle-class way of life. He was feeling good and doing well, but we both noticed that he was working obsessively—he had no off button. Some said he was now addicted to work. He was *overusing* his strengths, and we discussed ways to manage his success. He took a yoga class so he could learn more about meditation. What had been missing in his life was balance, and Jordan took to yoga like a fish to water. He made friendships and met women, and cautiously started dating. He tried several studios and, between AA and the yoga community, he gathered a great deal of support for sustainable well-being.

Over the span of about three years, Jordan had gone from being nearly hopeless to living an engaged life full of hope. When we are engaged in a life we have crafted, one that is aligned with our strengths, then meaning and purpose will naturally follow to carry us through any challenges.

Spending time evaluating and assessing what it would be like to be in this successful space can evoke strength. With embodied cognition, the roles and physical features that go with these changes can be power resources for recalling and strengthening your new identity. As you move toward the pull in your life, you'll want to regularly take the advice of the beat poet Allen Ginsberg: "Remember the future."[116]

As we do this, it is time to look at perhaps the most powerful of all the decisions we can make: to cherish relationships in our lives.

CHAPTER 8

Cherishing Relationships

"We've got this gift of love, but love is like a precious plant. You can't just accept it and leave it in the cupboard or just think it's going to get on by itself. You've got to keep watering it. You've got to really look after it and nurture it."

—*John Lennon*

Remember Stacey from Chapter 2? Her attitude on the first day she saw me was: "Who's going to want to date a forty-two-year-old with two kids and no money?" She believed that her circumstances were unchangeable and that the inevitable changes she was facing were a threat. She felt hopeless about her situation. I want to update you on how she did.

Stacey was right about her husband, Tom. He revealed himself to be mean-spirited and used the legal system to cause Stacey pain and suffering. He wasn't gracious with the divorce and had to be challenged through the court system at every turn. He had the most minimal contact with the children, and it became clear that his narcissistic tendencies and the fact he was a partner in his firm made him feel invincible and entitled—a dangerous combination.

Throughout the divorce, Stacey focused on her job as a fourth-grade teacher and her children. To address her fixed mindset of uncertainty and negativity, we put a plan together about what she could do. We focused on moving through the material you've been reading in this book, which included drawing on relationships for support.

She had magnificent friends at work and from college, and we put together a network of support so she could call them when Tom did something hurtful. Then I asked her to say "hello" to one new person a day. She hated this but did it, and the small act of saying hello allowed Stacey to become less of a shut-in. After the first month she was no longer put off by it. It became a positive habit for her, and she made it a practice to grow her circle of friends.

Tom's antics continued until one day an email to him at his office got bounced back with a note that he no longer worked at the firm. Tom's affair had been with one of the paralegals, who brought charges of harassment against him. Apparently, she wasn't the only affair he'd been having, and his partners had him removed.

Stacey headed for her lawyer's office to talk about the impact this would have on her, and on the way stopped at her favorite coffee shop. The line was unusually long. She said "hello" to the man behind her, and they chatted on the way to the cash register. When she went to pay for her coffee with her usual credit card, it was declined. They tried it again—declined again. Tom had cut off the funds.

She had no cash and was embarrassed, but the man she'd struck up the conversation with offered to buy her coffee. She thanked him, and they sat and talked. As it turned out, he was a widower with a chain of restaurants up and down the East Coast, and was assessing properties for a potential restaurant site. Two years later, they married in Hawaii. Stacey's efforts to stay connected amidst her depression opened a door to her future.

Perhaps you are feeling that your depression has been keeping you isolated, preventing you from connecting to others. Johann Hari, journalist and investigator of the causes of depression, has found that it's the other way around: isolation *causes* depression. In his book *Lost*

Connections,[117] he reviews the research on depression and finds relationship-building to be the pathway out. From everything we've seen about how the science of learned hopefulness works, this makes sense. It's clear that the primary focus for sustainable recovery is cultivating positive relationships.

Relationship Quality Is Closely Linked with Health and Well-Being

If depression has drained your energy, then the idea of trying to develop friendships and relationships may seem to be too distant to make happen. Yet in the midst of those feelings, it's important to know what science is finding about the effects of good relationships on our health.

A long and ongoing study has been analyzing the health and lives of the participants for decades—looking at what creates accomplishments and failures in careers and marriages. It began in 1938, during the Great Depression, with 268 Harvard sophomores, and by 2017, only nineteen participants were still alive. The data clearly debunks many of the elements thought to make life better, like how much money you have, and where—or if—you went to college. These things do not necessarily lead to a happy life. What *does* matter is the quality of our relationships.[118]

Robert Waldinger, the current director of the study, says, "The surprising finding is that our relationships and how happy we are in our relationships has a powerful influence on our health." He found that "The people who were the most satisfied in their relationships at age fifty were the healthiest at age eighty."[119] The vibrant psychiatrist George E. Vaillant, who navigated this study as its director for forty-two years, offers an even more precise summary:[120] "Happiness is love. Full stop."

Gratitude for Relationships

Most things you've learned about the seven decisions that facilitate or limit hope demonstrate how your perspective can change and refocus. This is true for your relationships as well. In this chapter, we will explore ways to refocus positively on past, present, and future relationships, which will in turn help you build skills and make connections. This is one of the things that will benefit you most in avoiding relapse. Relationships are often a major part of the cause for people to slip into a depression. They can also be the way out.

To begin, let's go back and look at people in your life who have been kind to you, showed you love, or were there for you in some way, and whom you may not have adequately thanked. This could include someone who is still in your life now, someone you've lost contact with, or someone who may have passed on.

Exploration: Virtual Gratitude Visit[121]

As you've done with the consult of your kind self exercise, set up two chairs across from one another. They can be the same or different, and as close or as far apart as you like. One chair will be for you, and the other will be where you'll imagine seating the person you have gratitude for. Once you imagine him or her in the chair, you can adjust your chair again. You may want to use a voice recorder for this exercise, and you will certainly want to have your journal.

Step 1: Begin in your chair and take a moment to imagine the person you'll express your gratitude to. Imagine him or her sitting there in the way they'd usually sit. Express your gratitude toward them as if you were speaking directly to them—even if they have passed on. Take your time and tell them all the things you are grateful for.

This exercise will help you integrate lost positive feelings, and in so doing it's not uncommon for many other emotions to emerge. This is normal. Tears are more often than not about the realization of our depth of gratitude—not necessarily sadness.

Step 2: Reverse roles and become the person you are expressing gratitude toward. Take a moment and be in their shoes. Sit like they would sit and imagine how they might feel if they had just heard you express your gratitude toward them. Respond, as them, in the way that makes the most sense.

Step 3: Change back into your seat and, if there's anything else you'd like to say to that person, say it now.

Immediately after doing this exercise, write down your thoughts, feelings, and insights. Take a moment to tap into how your body is feeling and how you are integrating this experience. As we've done previously, take a moment to notice what shifts may have taken place in your body. Record as much of your experience as feels right, and pay particular attention to what it was like to play both yourself and the other person.

The virtual gratitude visit, or VGV, grew out of my initial work with positive psychology and was built on one of the very first positive psychology interventions, designed by Marty Seligman.[122] He had students write a letter of gratitude and deliver it to someone personally. The research showed that not only did the letter writer's happiness scores go up, their scores on depression were lowered for at least a month following the exercise. This was one of the first positive interventions that demonstrated that an intentional act of well-being had a lasting wellness effect beyond the exercise itself.

As you may recall from Chapter 1, writing a letter of gratitude to someone is something I encourage. An email or even just a texted thank-you is typically a win-win. You'll feel good for having done it and they'll enjoy receiving it.

The VGV expands the impact of this method by integrating the feelings of receiving the gratitude. It also expands the potential experience of gratitude beyond those who are presently available.

Small Steps to Building Relationships

When we've been isolated in depression, trying to focus on relationships of any kind can be daunting. Each of the preceding chapters has provided tools to begin an upward spiral of energy. Although these are micro-shifts in the practice of applying these skills, they add up.

Just like many of the other strategies we've introduced, starting small is an excellent way to go with relationships as well. Major decisions like selling a house, getting divorced, and leaving a job can be draining, but the smaller daily decisions within them can be positive, so as not to rob you of precious mental energy.

Each day, it helps to make one small decision to relate to people. Let's begin with the people you know.

Exploration: Creating Your Social Atom

For this exercise, you'll need a blank sheet of paper in your journal. Using circles for females and triangles for males, place yourself anywhere on the sheet and put your first name in the middle of the symbol—a Social Atom.

Step 1: Draw everyone in your life now, with their symbol, and place it as close to/far away from you, as large or as small, as you want. These can be positive or negative relationships. There are no right or wrong ways to do this. If your aunt is geographically far away yet very positively meaningful to you, you might have her symbol far away from yours but large. Place in relative size and distance everyone who is in your life. If someone has passed on, you can make their symbol with dotted lines.

Step 2: Of the people on this Social Atom, identify one person with whom you'd be willing to increase your connection. Think about the various ways to do this and pick one. Could it be a text, a call, or a visit? Might you send an email or a card? Find one way to extend your contact. Perhaps you already see this person once a month; consider seeing him or her twice a month. Find a way to expand contact with the people you would like to have more in your life. Deepening our present connections is a good way to enhance well-being.

Give yourself thirty days to act on these decisions. Once you have, use your journal to note how increasing these connections has been helpful.

Step 3: Having more hope in our lives not only means more contact and connection with those that we have a positive association with already, it also means reducing the connection with people who drag our energy down and drain us. Go back and look at your Social Atom again. Who has a negative influence on you? What could you do to reduce the contact you are having with them? Note in particular those who have a large negative influence on you and with whom you have a high degree of contact. Think of ways of limiting the frequency with which you connect.

If hope is about the expectation of control over the future, just planning to spend less time with the people who drain you generates hope, all by itself. Try to carry this plan out within thirty days as well, and make entries in your journal about the experience.

The VGV warmed you up to relationships from your past that have been helpful, while the Social Atom gave you a quick glance at your family, friends, and "frenemies"—the not-so-helpful ones. Doing this exercise and then putting it into operation gives us back a sense of control. Adding action to the plan further feeds hope.

In our brains, we have a protein called brain-derived neurotrophic factor (BDNF)—which has been called "Miracle Grow for the brain"[123]—that has an extraordinary influence in easing depression and also seems to increase the brain's neuroplasticity, which helps protect and repair our brain while promoting better sleep. One of the biggest inhibitors of BDNF is social isolation. This is why being around people is so important.

This last exercise is one of the easiest ways to stimulate the production of BDNF. In Canada, the United Kingdom, Netherlands, Australia, and New Zealand, exercise is the first-line defense against depression—and only if that doesn't work will medication and therapy follow.[124] The studies show that one of the primary reasons exercise works is because it produces BDNF. Going to a gym or health club can help in two ways: you are around like-minded people, taking action through exercise; and, if you join a class, you increase your opportunities for social engagement—a vital goal.

Exploration: Expanding the Tribe

Step 1: In your journal, write down the three most important people in your life who are not blood relatives. This doesn't have to be about good influences only, just the people who've influenced your life the most. Chances are they have already shown up in an earlier exercise in this chapter, but you can use them again here. For our purpose, please limit it to three. It could be a spouse, a lover, a friend, a coworker, or a boss.

With each person, take a moment and write down how you met. Just a sentence or two. Recall the circumstances of your meeting and write them down.

Step 2: Once you've written this all down, you'll likely learn that each of the most influential people in your life you met by chance. Something other than direct planning brought you together. Think back to Stacey's story. The randomness of being in the coffee line and saying "hello," and her not having money, all aligned for the meeting to happen. The confluence of forces needed to make all of that happen are staggering—but one thing is certain: Stacey could not have made it happen; she could only do her part in getting ready for life to happen. Now it is your turn to do yours.

In order to begin making connections, you need to be where the people are. Think of places nearby where people congregate: the beach, a coffee shop, a university campus, the local park, or a shopping mall. Once you are there, I encourage you to deliberately expand your connection to others. I understand the difficulty, but I can also guarantee that whatever fear is keeping you from experimenting with connecting has been blown out of proportion by the negative thinking behind the depression. The fear can change almost instantly if you make a different decision.

Perhaps one of the easiest and least intrusive ways to make a connection is to smile at someone. I have often been amazed at how a simple smile can cause a positive reaction. Later in the chapter I will talk more about positivity resonance, but for now it's enough to know that having a smile returned to you can be a very simple yet powerful way to exercise some control over your expectations. This isn't just a nicety; there is some good science that shows that smiling can activate positive responses in others[125]—not to mention help change your own thought processes. Not everyone will respond, but if one person doesn't, the next one might. You'll probably get enough positive responses to feel like you initiated a brief but positive connection with someone.

Here are some other ways to engage. Again, you may find that your hit rate is about 50 percent—but that's 50 percent more people you've connected to. Here are some more ideas.

- Say "hello" to someone in a queue with you, as Stacey did.

- Ask a stranger a question. ("How often do the buses run from here?")

- Ask for directions from someone you don't know. ("I'm trying to get to the theater. Do you know where it is?")

- Compliment what someone is wearing. ("Great hat!")

- Comment on a shared experience ("The food here is delicious, isn't it?")

- Admire a tattoo. ("That's interesting; did you design it yourself?")

- Ask for suggestions. ("I'm new to this area. Can you tell me a good place for lunch?")

These are all ways to initiate a connection. Depression and social isolation work hand in hand to deplete us and keep hope from happening. As difficult or uncomfortable as it might feel to make contact with others, it is the most direct way to pull you out of depression's vortex. Think of it as a powerful medicine that might not taste good, but it works. It's simply part of what needs to be done to get better.

Practice stretching yourself in this way, until it becomes a regular habit. It usually begins to feel more natural after a month, and to become part of your routine after two. This is worth taking a risk to do. Be sure to write down your experiences in your journal.

The next step on this path is sharing an experience with other people. This is different than being around people walking by you in a park—we're talking more like an organized event. Going to a seminar, a talk, or a workshop brings you together with like-minded people, and the opportunity for engagement goes up. You are more than with people—you are sharing an experience together, which gives you a common occurrence to talk about. Commenting on the experience or asking questions is often an easy way to begin to connect. Being at an event where everyone has just shared an experience, combined with your new skills of engagement, can open up many possibilities.

The next level is looking for meetups, clubs, classes, etc. When you are regularly connected to a group by interest and discussion, and when socializing is typically encouraged, many factors stack the deck in favor of you making connections. Sometimes having a supportive environment will help reduce or remove your inhibitions. Taking a class, doing an intensive seminar, anything that gives you repeated connections with the same people, will be good. These actions may be the most dynamic and far-reaching ways to undo the elements of depression.

Twelve-step programs are also good examples: social networks of people working together toward feeling better. The steps are just part of the healing—in the long run, it is the repeated fellowship and sharing with others that help the most.

Expanding What Love Is

Can saying hello to someone in your yoga class or someone you meet in line at Starbucks really be critical in uncoupling from your depression? Barbara Fredrickson thinks so. In her book *Love 2.0,* she challenges us to reinterpret the biochemistry of love and the power of connecting to strangers. Love isn't only about romance and sexual attraction. She refers to this limited notion of love as a "worldwide collapse of imagination."[126] She believes that these moments of positivity resonance are the same whether they're between parent and child, friends, lovers, or total strangers. These experiences are, in her words, biochemically "virtually identical."

According to this view, evolution has designed us to love as a means of survival. Dr. Fredrickson calls this a positivity resonance, and it is our job to find as many ways of activating that resonance as possible. Any moment of shared positivity increases this connection—which can spark an upward spiral. The risk of attempting these connections may feel high, but it is actually quite low. A shared nod and smile to a fellow human being may take some courage, but it's not a life or death situation. Taking a risk to make a connection might be the best tool you have for not experiencing social isolation and risking a depression relapse.

This is your challenge. Say hello to someone new each day. The first week is difficult, but over time it becomes a new habit that allows greater ease in moving out into the world. I encourage you to keep notes in your journal about your progress. As you get more comfortable with this, you can use the other suggestions above to keep making connections.

Resetting Familiar Routes Through Life

The reason these changes are difficult is because we are usually going up against patterns of behavior that have taken a long time to evolve. In attachment theory, which explains how infants bond to their parents and caregivers, there's something called *synchronization* and *desynchronization.* When we are in tune with a caregiver, we are in sync—and Barbara Fredrickson's research demonstrates that positive emotions breed synchrony. Depression does not.

While this is true, something happens to our internal GPS system when we've been in a depression for a while, or if we grew up with people who were depressed. Our ability to navigate life gets thrown off. In a depression, we may have been making choices that keep us away from hope for so long that depression itself becomes a habitual pattern. In other words, it may feel like we are in sync when we do things to keep us depressed—and out of sync if we do something different. Your internal GPS may be pointing you toward the wrong destination.

One of the most consistent findings in infant development research is the infant's preference for the familiar. Human infants have a powerful ability to recognize something they have seen before. Evolutionary psychologists point out that an infant's ability to do this has survival value. Recognizing and making eye contact with caretakers increases the likelihood that you'll be fed and taken care of. Spotting a dangerous incident—like fire—means you'll remember to avoid it.

But this power of recognition goes far beyond remembering a specific thing. Infants can remember something familiar. The root of the words "family" and "familiar" are the same. Infants are drawn to something—or someone—familiar because it makes them feel safe (even if it isn't). It isn't about good and bad so much as it is about familiar and unfamiliar. When infants are given a one-inch ball to play with for a brief time, then given a one-inch cube and a one-inch ball, they will always choose the ball, because it's familiar. But in the same experiment, if an infant is given a one-inch ball and then shown a three-inch ball and a three-inch cube—they still choose the ball, even though they have not seen either of the three-inch objects before. This shows the miracle of the human brain to form prototypes. They choose the three-inch ball because it's the most like the one-inch ball they played with.

The same happens with our emotions. When we are used to feeling a certain way, depressed, we seem to find ways to maintain that depression. We sit on the couch rather than go for a walk. We'll stay caught in our thinking and acting traps because they are familiar. We stay isolated rather than connect. This is also why you hear, for better or worse, that someone "married their mother." Or their father. We are drawn to the familiar, and the psyche doesn't care so much about good and bad—it cares more about the same and different. That is why changing the patterns of our depression is so hard. We are being drawn to continue doing what we've always done, and trying something different feels unfamiliar—and as a result, difficult.

I believe Barbara Fredrickson is right when she says that positive emotions breed synchrony. They return us to a natural state—not the habitual one we've developed around depression. In working with many people who have come from highly dysfunctional families, it seems as if they are drawn to the same type of dynamics found in their family of origin. Giving them some new positive experiences and helping them make better decisions facilitates hope that something better can happen than what they've experienced.

This is what you can do with your depression too. You can engage with more positive experiences, which will not only contrast with the experiences you've had, but keep you from isolating from people—who are the strongest source of hope.

Kintsugi: The Art of Precious Scars[127]

I've never met a person who hasn't been hurt in a relationship. To be human is to feel the pain that comes from rejection, betrayal, or loss. Suffering in this way is part of being alive—but what we do with that suffering is up to us. As Wayne Dyer has put it: "How people treat you is their karma; how you react is yours."

The Japanese art of *kintsugi* ("golden repair") teaches that broken objects should not be discarded, but rather repaired and displayed with pride. In this practice, breaks in the ceramic bowl, teapot, or other pottery are highlighted with the use of a precious metal. Usually, liquid gold or liquid silver is applied, to repair the item while simultaneously enhancing the breaks. Joining the fragments in this way elevates the repaired piece to a unique work of art. The randomness of the break creates new patterns in the piece, enhanced through the use of precious metals.

Social isolation is the break in the pottery of our life, and connecting to others is liquid gold. When we are fragmented, our isolation from others becomes a source feeding our depression. Putting our lives back together happens best when we learn how to reach out to others. As you continue the process of connection, you may find that you want to repair one or two relationships. The effort to repair something can make it more valuable than it was originally. Repairing what is ruptured can make it beautiful in ways that weren't possible before.

Even if it is not possible to repair a specific relationship, expanding your tribe by relating to new people is healing. Developing new relationships and connections is the liquid gold that helps put our lives back together. Learning from negativity, shifting our perspective to the positive, and recognizing that we have a choice about how we perceive our situation is learned hopefulness. Connections to other people make each of our lives a unique work of art.

Expressing Positivity to Maintain Relationships

In relationship science, earlier work focused on much the same as general psychology—on what's wrong with a relationship. What was working was dismissed to emphasize correction and repair. In this chapter, you've been learning tools of connection, finding ways to connect with others. Now let's look at how to maintain relationships.

Relationship scientists like John Gottman and Shelly Gable noticed that the expressed positivity within a relationship is very important, both for predicting how good and long a relationship would last, and for determining how it could be strengthened. Shelly Gable[128] has put forth research showing that our celebration of others' good news is one ticket to better relationships.

When we're locked inside our own depression and isolation, we become consumed with the negativity of our own thoughts, feelings, and losses. It's like we've constructed a wall to keep us safe. But what protects us also inhibits us. The focus is on what we don't or can't have, and others' needs are distant or unknown to us. By keeping to ourselves, the ties to others and their good fortune is absent. An act of kindness, as noted earlier, is one of the quickest ways to get out of the quicksand of depression. It may also be the most important predictor of a great marriage.[129] The moment you are thinking about someone else's needs, you have broken out of the thinking and acting traps keeping you stuck.

Shelly Gable has boiled down the styles of responding to four possibilities: active constructive, active destructive, passive destructive, and passive constructive.

In active constructive responding, you are responding to someone else's good fortune, in a celebration and expression of joy for them. In essence, you are allowing the person to relive their experience of having received their good news, through showing your excitement for them. It's almost as if you are interviewing them about what has made them happy. Think of it as a scientific investigation of sorts— you are looking for more joy in your life, and this person has found something that has brought that to them. In the developing field of positive psychotherapy, this is one of the central skills taught to participants; it's part of a collection of interventions, most of which you are learning in this book, that have been shown to directly reduce depression and increase well-being in a sustainable way.

At the other end of the spectrum is passive constructive. Someone tells you they get a big promotion, and you say, "That's nice." It's the ultimate buzzkill for them—and also distances you from the positive experience, by not taking interest. If you want to feel better, then you need to support others. But when we are depressed, mild statements may be all we think we can offer. This is another way of strengthening your trap. If your level of engagement and enthusiasm doesn't match theirs, they are much less likely to share good news with you in the future, and unlikely to respond to your accomplishments with any excitement.

In a passive-destructive response, you respond to the other's good news with good news of your own. You usurp their enthusiasm by matching it with your own. In this scenario, if someone gets a new car and is very happy about it, you respond with your enthusiasm for the condo you're buying. This passive-destructive response takes the wind out of their sails and their good news goes unrecognized.

Finally, there is active-destructive responding. Here you actually challenge the good news. Someone who just bought a new car they are excited about is met with your response that it is a gas-guzzler, or that it's expensive to maintain. While these things may be true, they undo the other person's positivity.

Over the next week, record in your journal each time you were able to respond to someone else's good news. Be conscious and deliberate about this and find ways to get them to relive their experience with you. By embracing the good fortune of others, you'll be enriching your own.

Now you are ready to pull all of this together and create a plan to maintain the changes you've made with learned hopefulness. As you'll see in our final chapter, the key to maintaining progress is continuing to learn.

CHAPTER 9

Living the Life You Imagine

"Eventually it became clear that our emotions, attitudes, and thoughts profoundly affect our bodies, sometimes to the degree of life or death. Soon mind–body effects were recognized to have positive as well as negative impacts on the body. This realization came largely from research on the placebo effect—the beneficial results of suggestion, expectation, and positive thinking."

—*Larry Dossey*

Medical and psychological communities use the placebo effect to measure the effectiveness of treatment—it's what the drug companies have to beat in order to be considered effective. The beneficial effect of a placebo is due to the patient's *belief* in the treatment alone. Remember: beliefs change expectations, which influences outcome.

When a drug doesn't do better than the placebo, *the study doesn't get published.* In what is known as *publication bias,* only the studies showing that a drug beat the placebo get into the journals. This means that if there are a hundred studies and ninety-eight of them don't show any effect, the scientific community only reads about the two that show the effectiveness of the drug—not the ninety-eight that show the efficacy of the placebo.[130]

The power of the placebo effect is the very thing you've been learning about in this book. Noted physician Herbert Spiegel says,

"The placebo effect can occur when conditions are optimal for hope, faith, trust, and love." Dr. Irving Kirsch, a leading authority studying clinical trials of antidepressants by drug companies, looked at the results and found that nearly 80 percent of the effectiveness of antidepressants can be attributed to the placebo effect. What we *believe* influences our well-being more than the chemical being given. According to a *New York Times* article: "The critical factor," Kirsch says, "is our beliefs about what's going to happen to us. You don't have to rely on drugs to see profound transformation."[131]

Beliefs alone can change results, and this is perhaps most notable in the work of positive psychotherapy. This strength-based approach began with the belief that people can improve their well-being, not just alleviate their suffering. Studies were done by Tayyab Rashid and Marty Seligman using positive interventions (similar to the ones we've been exploring); they showed that the outcomes for depression beat the treatment as usual (TAU) psychotherapies for depression, *and* the TAU plus antidepressants.[132]

Why? Because the interventions create *positive expectations*— beliefs about what's going to happen to us. In turn, these positive expectations create very positive results. In one study, the effectiveness of positive psychotherapy was nearly *three* times greater than typical psychotherapy and antidepressants combined. When people practice their belief that they can have more hope and well-being in their life, the results are powerful. As Dr. Joe Dispenza has said, *You Are the Placebo*,[133] and you've been learning similar skills and practices in this book, to make better decisions that shift your expectations.

If I could offer one sentence to sum up this book, it would be: *Hope doesn't change what we believe—what we believe changes how we hope.* In Chapter 1, I shared the metaphor of light as it passes through a prism and changes into a full spectrum of color. Cultivating intentional well-being is changing the beliefs that filter our choices. By addressing the beliefs, we can challenge the decisions we have been making to empower ourselves to make different choices.

There is a hierarchy to how hope functions that gives us a way of dealing with the negativity and uncertainty that inevitably arise in life. Let's look at how this process works.

Hierarchy of Hope

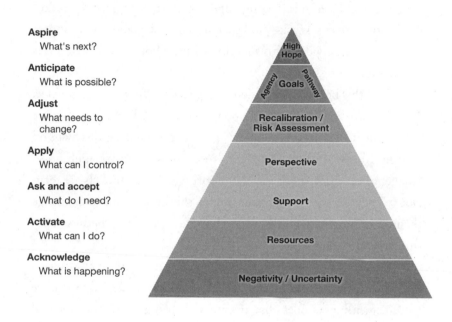

Aspire
What's next?

Anticipate
What is possible?

Adjust
What needs to change?

Apply
What can I control?

Ask and accept
What do I need?

Activate
What can I do?

Acknowledge
What is happening?

Perspective, what this book has been about, and what you've been working to shift, is in the middle of the hierarchy. It is the tipping point in the system because it focuses on our beliefs about what we can control or influence. Each layer in the hierarchy of hope gives us a question to consider and a course of action that follows. Since negativity and uncertainty are the necessary ingredients in activating hope, they are at the base.

"What is happening?" is the first question we need to ask ourselves when there is negativity and uncertainty in a situation. This question is designed to help us acknowledge our state of affairs more clearly—to deal with what is, rather than what we assume. Rather than being clouded by denial or misinformation, an honest appraisal lets us more accurately answer the question "What can I do?" This allows us to activate the resources needed. Once we have accurately assessed our situation, we can then ask ourselves what is at our disposal for remedying it.

Depression thrives on isolation. To directly counteract this, the next essential layer in activating hope is getting support. "What do I need?" prompts us to ask—and then accept—the emotional support required. Not only does this support cultivate hope, but it also limits the fuel for depression.

All of this bring us to the doorstep of controlling our perspective. "What can I control?" gives us power because it highlights that we are making a decision. As you now know, the seven decisions focus on shifting from old habits of thought to those in line with high hope. Challenging old perspectives takes effort because old beliefs are tenacious. They become our default way of thinking—and to challenge them is to loosen their grip. The thoughts are strong because they think they are protecting us.

In each of the explorations, you engaged in intentional activities designed to awaken alternative choices and replace the old protective patterns with new ones that inspire well-being. The new ways of thinking protect us in a better way, and you've proven to yourself throughout the book that they can be effective. When you challenge an old habit of thought, you begin the process of emotional self-regulation. *The effort to change is the change itself.* By attempting to challenge your decisions, you're self-regulating. You're intentionally addressing the direction of your thought; instead of leaving the old direction of thought unchallenged, you've considered an alternative. Imagine a corrupt leader, unopposed for a long time, suddenly challenged by alternative leadership. By giving voters a choice—a decision to be made—there is empowerment. You can choose a new leader or put the old one back in power. If you put the old habits of thought back in power once you know there is an alternative, at least you'll know they are there because a decision has been made.

Further up the hierarchy is the link between the seven decisions: recalibration and risk assessment through goal-setting. When we initially recalibrate our goal (remember Anne's story about washing one dish) to link to high hope, it pulls us into the process of recalibrating and risk assessment. To maintain hope means we must continually monitor our goals and risks. This means "What needs to change?" becomes our relentless mantra. Think of the surfer who has caught the wave. Now they have to use other skills to ride it and maintain balance; their goals and risk assessment work hand in hand to move them forward. Once Anne felt empowered by washing one dish, she made a different risk assessment of her other goals and started tackling them. "What needs to change?" became her newfound mantra.

Toward the top of the hierarchy, we can see the original cluster of concepts used by one of the pioneering theorists in hope. Agency, pathway, and goals leading to high hope are built upon the foundation leading to them. Just as an archeologist discovering the top of a previous finding, further exploration reveals the entire treasure. Pulling together what other researchers have found supports this notion and the question "What's possible?" This is where high hope lives. High hope develops when empowerment from our ability to change perspective becomes a tipping point: when we move toward our next set of goals by asking, "What's next?" rather than "Why me?" as a response to our pain.

The Power of *Belief* Modification

In the 1960s, there was a large, strong movement toward *behavior modification.* This branch of psychology was founded on the simple notion that we are drawn toward what we want and will avoid what is painful and unwanted. For decades, this view dominated the approach to helping individuals change, and was the darling of interventions for teachers, parents, therapists, and business leaders.

Behavior modification is based on the principles of reinforcement and punishment. When you want someone to repeat a behavior, you reinforce it by giving them what they want, or stopping something unpleasant. If a parent wants their child to clean their room, they could promise their kid twenty dollars *and* to stop nagging them if they do it. (I'm not recommending this—just an example!) This uses positive reinforcement (the twenty dollars) and negative reinforcement (stop nagging) to modify the child's behavior. The positive is given, and the negative reinforcement is removed. If the parent wanted to add something else to help change the behavior, they could punish the opposite actions of the child: when they don't clean their room, they lose their allowance.

Behavior modification was somewhat successful and important in helping people change, but flawed in many ways because the controlling agent (person) is outside the individual whose behavior is being modified. When we tried to use these principles to help people with depression, they didn't work in the same way. Feeling better should have been a positive reinforcer, feeling depressed should have been a negative reinforcer, and isolation should have felt like a punishment (this is why prisons use solitary confinement as a penalty). But instead, people chose depression over feeling better and isolation over connection. Why? Because what is needed is a *belief* modification.

To understand belief modification and how it might impact a depression, let me return to the research on the placebo effect for a moment to look at the other side: *the nocebo effect.*[134] This effect happens when we consider the negative beliefs about something, causing a negative reaction.

The most prominent example of this is the side effects of antide-pressants. In a comprehensive analysis of 143 studies on the nocebo effect, patients *who did not get an antidepressant* demonstrated differ-ent levels of side effects for the different classes of drugs.[135] People thinking they were getting one type of antidepressant, a tricyclic, had higher reports of dry mouth, vision problems, fatigue, and constipa-tion than if they were told they were taking an SSRI (selective sero-tonin reuptake inhibitor). They experienced the type and degree of side effects based on what they were told to experience. *Neither* group was receiving *any* antidepressant, yet they reported different levels of side effects based on expectation alone!

With depression, we are creating our own nocebo effect by *expect-ing things not to get better*. Depression is the side effect of believing, and then expecting. It isn't going to change because we have no control over it. As soon as we believe we have some control—it changes. To take liberties with Dr. Spiegel's quote earlier in this chapter: "The nocebo effect can occur when conditions are optimal for despair, disbelief, distrust, and dislike."

If you've ever Googled the side effects of a drug, you probably wished you hadn't. Once we think something bad can happen, it changes our expectations. When we are depressed, it's as if we are Googling what can go wrong and then believing that is our future. But this doesn't have to be the case. As Allen Ginsberg reminds us, "everyone wants to feel, and wants to feel loved and to love, so there is inevitable Hope beneath every grim mask."[136]

All of the work in this book has been targeted at helping you unshackle from the negative effects of depression. We've been approaching its symptoms as habits stemming from beliefs that limit our sense of hope. Habit experts tell us that we can set goals to change the outcome (what we hope to achieve), the process (the means to get there), or our identity (how we think of ourselves). In his book *Atomic Habits*,[137] author James Clear explains that "Habits are the compound interest of self-improvement." I think that's true if the habits are good ones.

However, if they lead to depression, then these negative habits *become the account withdrawals of emotional bankruptcy.* This reiterates how habits, particularly habits of thought and action, can profoundly influence our lives—one way or the other. The power of a habit is in its ability to strengthen intention. Each of the exploration exercises has emphasized that high-hope beliefs are needed to shape our habits of thought. They give you skills to not only change perspective but to practice shifting toward that perspective, moving forward.

Never Miss a Day

To form high-hope beliefs, you'll have to be as relentless as your depression. Regardless of what else is going on, your depression was always operating in the background, waiting to trip you up by making you feel hopeless about the future. To overcome this habit, you'll want to be prepared with your toolbox of new skills, to untangle from what held you back in the past, become more present, and have positive expectations for the future. As Dr. Bruce Lipton has explained,[138] "Once you become aware that you are responsible for your thoughts, you are responsible for your thoughts."

How do you begin this process? You check in with yourself every day to make sure you are doing something toward intentional wellbeing. As an example, when I wake up in the morning, I often begin with a gratitude review from the day before. This starts me on my path for the day with a positive perspective, shifting from my default for my thoughts and paying attention to the more positive ones.

Exploration: Keeping a Skills Chart

The more tools we have, the more skills we develop when we use them. As you are getting ready to continue the practice of these skills, it's useful to create a chart of them. Then you can mark a calendar on every day you apply one of the tools and consider marking with a special color on a day you learned a new tool. As an example, if you've discovered that physical exercise is a great way to combat depression and increase your well-being (which it is) and you take your first yoga class—put that down in a special color.

This strategy is based on what's sometimes called the *Seinfeld productivity hack*. Comedian Jerry Seinfeld apparently marked his calendar with a big "X" every day he came up with a joke. Soon, his goal became not to break the series, and this was his advice to start-up comics: Never miss a day. Now, this is my advice to you.

As time goes on, you'll find many things that will not only keep depression at bay but also add to greater life satisfaction and joy. New meditations, foods, physical activities, creative explorations, positive interventions, social activities, and music are just a small sample that can all be sources of your broaden-and-build process.

You've done the work. You are changing your life for the better. I admire the journey you've chosen and hope I can be a help to you as we go forward together. Let's continue; hope is happening.

Acknowledgments

There were many times in writing this book about hope that I was uncertain. As you've learned, these feelings are essential for hope to be ignited. Also essential are people who provide wisdom through their support, guidance, and inspiration. When I brought my murky concerns to my friends, family, or colleagues, their light illuminated the way. I can only hope to do for others what they've done for me.

The editorial staff at New Harbinger—from. Wendy Millstine and Jennye Garibaldi, acquisitions editors, to Jennifer Holder, coordinating and developmental editor, as well as Clancy Drake and Teja Watson—have been extraordinary. At every turn, their encouragement, suggestions, and concerns have improved my writing and given form and substance to my ideas. To these wonderful guardians of the written word I extend my deepest gratitude.

Martin Seligman's life work and global influence have captured the attention of scientists, educators, business leaders, medical practitioners, coaches, therapists, the military, and the imagination of people everywhere —and for good reason. His penetrating insights, research acumen, and pioneering spirit have changed how we view the well-being of the world. I have been lucky to have studied with Marty and to have served as his assistant since 2012 in the Master of Applied Positive Psychology (MAPP) program at UPenn. He has allowed me to grow personally and professionally in ways I could not have imagined—and to Marty I am beyond grateful.

James Pawelski—professor of practice, director of education, MAPP program at UPenn—is a mentor and exemplar. I've also been lucky enough to serve as James's assistant in his humanities course in the MAPP program since 2012. James's attention to detail as a writer, his openness as a teacher, and his grace as a communicator have been a constant source of inspiration.

The MAPP community is far beyond the normal academic program of study, and since 2011, as a student, I've had instructors, colleagues, and friends who continually support, challenge, and nurture my development as a writer and a person. Leona Brandwene, Johannes Eichstaedt, Dan Bowling, Dan Lerner, Reb and Amy Rebele, Elaine O'Brien, Jennifer Cory, Jordyn Feingold, Cory Muscara, Scott Asalone, Andrew Soren, Julia King, Sophia Kokores, Henry Edwards , Gloria Park, David Yaden, Anne Bradford, Emily Esfahani Smith, Suzann Pileggi Pawelski, Laura Taylor, Mary Bit Smith, Katheryn Britton, Lisa Sansom, Pete Berridge, Shannon Polly, Caroline Adams Miller, Louisa Jewels, Kunal Sood, Emilia Lahti, and Jan Stanley truly represent the essence of what has been called "the magic of MAPP." I am a better person for having each of them in my life.

Leaders in the field who have been beacons of light in carving a path of influence are Ryan Niemiec, Barbara Fredrickson, Bob Vallerand, Scott Barry Kaufman, Adam Grant, Angela Duckworth, Tal Ben-Shahar, Judy Saltzberg Levick, Tayyab Rashid, Joan Beasley, Nina Garcia, Bob and Jacquie Siroka, and Alan Schlechter.

At Teachers College, Columbia University, I am particularly indebted to Lisa Miller, founder of the Spirituality Mind Body Institute, Aurélie Athan, academic director and director of clinical training, and Randall Richardson, program director, Psychology in Education, Department of Counseling and Clinical Psychology, for their constant encouragement and support of experiential education in the classroom. Many of the firsthand explorations in this book were woven into the classroom experiences, and the feedback from the students has helped shape them into something accessible. In particular, Charly Jaffe has come through one of these classes and has been exceptionally helpful in pulling together the references for the endnotes.

Finally, there are those closest to me. Joel and Marilyn Morgovsky are lifelong friends whose presence in my life remains a constant treasure, as is Andrea Szucs, my love and muse, who practices and shares these principles of hope with me. My dynamic and inspiring daughter, Devon Tomasulo, and my dear son-in-law, Spencer, recently gave birth to my first grandson, Callahan Thomas Fetrow. It is such a joy to hold him and feel all the potential of what is to come. He represents what this book is all about: "wonder, hope, a dream of possibilities."

Endnotes

Foreword

1   E. P. Torrance, "The importance of falling in love with 'something,'" *Creative Child & Adult Quarterly, 8*(2) (1983) 72–78.

2   A. Maslow, *Toward a Psychology of Being* (New York: D. Van Nostrand Company, 1968).

Introduction

3   K. Sim, W. K. Lau, J. Sim, M. Y. Sum, and R. J. Baldessarini. "Prevention of Relapse and Recurrence in Adults with Major Depressive Disorder: Systematic Review and Meta-Analyses of Controlled Trials," *The International Journal of Neuropsychopharmacology* 19(2) (2015), https://dash.harvard.edu/bitstream/handle/1/26318628/4772815. (Recurrence rates are more than 85 percent within a decade of an index depressive episode, and average approximately 50 percent or more within six months of apparent clinical remission if the initially effective treatment was not continued.)

4   S. L. Burcusa and W. G. Iacono, "Risk for Recurrence in Depression," *Clinical Psychology Review* 27(8) (2007): 959–985, https://www.ncbi.nlm.nih.gov/pmc/articles/PMC2169519/pdf/nihms34016.pdf. "At least 50 percent of those who recover from a first episode of depression have one or more additional episodes in their lifetime, and approximately 80 percent of those with a history of two episodes have another recurrence."

5   T. Rashid and M. P. Seligman, *Positive Psychotherapy: Clinician Manual* (Oxford University Press, 2018).

6   G. A. Fava and C. Ruini, "Development and Characteristics of a Well-Being Enhancing Psychotherapeutic Strategy: Well-Being Therapy," *Journal of Behavior Therapy and Experimental Psychiatry* 34 (2003): 45–63. (This article describes the main characteristics and technical features of

a novel psychotherapeutic strategy, well-being therapy. This paper outlines the background of its development, structure, key concepts, and technical aspects.)

Chapter 1

7   M. E. P. Seligman, "Positive Psychology: A Personal History," *Annual Review of Clinical Psychology* 15(1) (2018): 23, http://www.annualreviews.org/doi/full/10.1146/annurev-clinpsy-050718-095653.

8   S. F. Maier and M. E. Seligman, "Learned Helplessness at Fifty: Insights from Neuroscience," *Psychological Review* 123(4) (2016): 349–367, https://www.ncbi.nlm.nih.gov/pcm/articles/PCM4920136/.

9   Ibid.

10   J. S. Cheavens, J. E. Heiy, D. B. Feldman, C. Benitez, and K. L. Rand, "Hope, Goals, and Pathways: Further Validating the Hope Scale with Observer Ratings," *The Journal of Positive Psychology* 14(4) (2019): 452–462.

11   B. L. Fredrickson, "Positive Emotions Broaden and Build," in *Advances in Experimental Social Psychology*, 47, ed. P. Devine and A. Plant (Burlington, MA: Academic Press, 2013): 1–53. (A review, comprehensive to date, of a fifteen-year research program on the broaden-and-build theory of positive emotions.)

12   K. Herth, "Abbreviated Instrument to Measure Hope: Development and Psychometric Evaluation," *Journal of Advanced Nursing* 17(10) (1992): 1251–1259. (The purpose of this research was to develop and evaluate psychometrically an abbreviated instrument to assess hope in adults in clinical settings.)

13   B. L. Fredrickson, "Positive Emotions Broaden and Build," in *Advances in Experimental Social Psychology*, 47, ed. P. Devine and A. Plant (Burlington, MA: Academic Press, 2013): 1–53.

14   C. J. Farran, K. A. Herth, and J. M. Popovich, *Hope and Hopelessness: Critical Clinical Constructs* (Thousand Oaks, CA: Sage Publications, Inc., 1995). (This book represents twenty-seven collective

years of work in the area of hope and hopelessness, with a focus on the positive aspects of hope and its relationship to health.)

15   B. L. Fredrickson, "The Role of Positive Emotions in Positive Psychology: The Broaden-and-Build Theory of Positive Emotions," *The American Psychologist* 56(3) (2001): 218–226. (The broaden-and-build theory posits that experience of positive emotions broadens people's momentary thought–action repertoires, which in turn serves to build their enduring personal resources, ranging from physical and intellectual resources to social and psychological resources.)

16   A. Vaish, T. Grossmann, and A. Woodward. "Not All Emotions Are Created Equal: The Negativity Bias in Social-Emotional Development," *Psychological Bulletin* 134(3) (2008): 383–403. (Across an array of psychological situations and tasks, adults display a negativity bias, or the propensity to attend to, learn from, and use negative information far more than positive information. The authors discuss ontogenetic mechanisms underlying the emergence of this bias and explore not only its evolutionary but also its developmental functions and consequences.)

17   S. F. Maier and M. E. Seligman, "Learned Helplessness at Fifty: Insights from Neuroscience," *Psychological Review* 123(4) (2016): 349–367.

18   M. E. P. Seligman, *Learned Optimism: How to Change Your Mind and Your Life* (New York: Vintage Books, 2006).

19   T. Rashid, "Positive Psychotherapy: A Strength-Based Approach," *The Journal of Positive Psychology* 10(1) (2015): 25–40.

20   K. A. Herth, "Development and Implementation of a Hope Intervention Program," *Oncology Nursing Forum* 28(6) (2001): 1009–1016. (This article describes the development and evaluation of the Hope Intervention Program, or HIP, designed to enhance hope, based on the Hope Process Framework.)

21   C. Feudner, "Hope and the Prospects of Healing at the End of Life," *The Journal of Alternative and Complementary Medicine* 11(1) (2005): 23–30. (This paper considers possible interventions and how

they might be evaluated, seeking to improve the prospects of healing at the end of life.)

22   A. Duckworth, *Grit: The Power of Passion and Perseverance* (New York: Scribner, 2016), 169.

23   B. L. Fredrickson, "The Role of Positive Emotions in Positive Psychology: The Broaden-and-Build Theory of Positive Emotions," *The American Psychologist* 56(3) (2001): 218–226.

24   B. Fredrickson, *Positivity: Top-Notch Research Reveals the 3 to 1 Ratio that Will Change Your Life* (New York: Harmony Books, 2009).

25   This was the premise of my play, *Negatively Oriented Therapy* (*NOT*).

26   S. Nolen-Hoeksema, B. E. Wisco, and S. Lyubomirsky, "Rethinking Rumination," *Perspectives on Psychological Science* 3(5) (2008): 400–424.

27   P. Zimbardo and J. Boyd, *The Time Paradox: The New Psychology of Time That Will Change Your Life* (New York: Simon and Schuster, 2008): 62.

28   E. Livni, "A Nobel Prize-Winning Psychologist Says Most People Don't Really Want to Be Happy," *Quartz*, December 21, 2018, https://qz.com/1503207/a-nobel-prize-winning-psychologist-defines-happiness-versus-satisfaction/.

29   S. C. Cramer, M. Sur, B. H. Dobkin, C. O'Brien, T. D. Sanger, J. Q. Trojanowski, et al., "Harnessing Neuroplasticity for Clinical Applications," *Brain* 134(6) (2011): 1591–1609.

30   P. Kini, J. Wong, S. McInnis, N. Gabana, and J. Brown, "The Effects of Gratitude Expression on Neural Activity," *NeuroImage* 128(2016): 1–10. (The study found that a simple gratitude writing intervention was associated with significantly greater and lasting neural sensitivity to gratitude—subjects who participated in gratitude letter writing showed both behavioral increases in gratitude and significantly greater neural modulation by gratitude in the medial prefrontal cortex three months later.)

31   A. M. Wood, J. Maltby, R. Gillett, P. A. Linley, and S. Joseph, "The Role of Gratitude in the Development of Social Support, Stress, and Depression: Two Longitudinal Studies," *Journal of Research in Personality* 42(4) (2008): 854–871. (Overall gratitude seems to directly foster social support and to protect people from stress and depression, which has implications for clinical interventions.)

32   C. S. Dweck, *Mindset: The New Psychology of Success* (New York: Random House, 2006).

33   T. Lomas, J. J. Froh, R. A. Emmons, A. Mishra, and G. Bono, *The Wiley Blackwell Handbook of Positive Psychological Interventions* (Hoboken, NJ: Wiley-Blackwell, 2014), 1.

34   M. E. P. Seligman, *Learned Optimism: How to Change Your Mind and Your Life* (New York: Vintage Books, 2006).

35   M. E. Seligman, T. A. Steen, N. Park, and C. Peterson, "Positive Psychology Progress: Empirical Validation of Interventions," *American Psychologist* 60(5) (2005): 410.

36   A. M. Grant and F. Gino, "A Little Thanks Goes a Long Way: Explaining Why Gratitude Expressions Motivate Prosocial Behavior," *Journal of Personality and Social Psychology* 98(6) (2010): 946–955. (The authors propose that gratitude expressions can enhance prosocial behavior through both agentic and communal mechanisms, such that when helpers are thanked for their efforts they experience stronger feelings of self-efficacy and social worth, which motivate them to engage in prosocial behavior.)

Chapter 2

37   C. S. Dweck, *Mindset: The New Psychology of Success* (New York: Random House, 2006).

38   M. L. Peters, I. K. Flink, K. Boersma, and S. J. Linton, "Manipulating Optimism: Can Imagining a Best Possible Self Be Used to Increase Positive Future Expectancies?," *The Journal of Positive Psychology* 5(3) (2010): 204–211. (Participants in the positive future

thinking condition wrote about their best possible self, or BPS, for fifteen minutes, followed by five minutes of mental imagery. The results indicate that imagining a positive future can indeed increase expectancies for a positive future.)

39   W. Cohen, *Drucker on Leadership: New Lessons from the Father of Modern Management* (San Francisco: Jossey-Bass, 2010): 4.

40   H. D. Thoreau, *Walden,* (New York: Thomas Crowell, 1910): 427.

41   M. L. Peters, Y. M. Meevissen, and M. M. Hanssen, "Specificity of the Best Possible Self Intervention for Increasing Optimism: Comparison with a Gratitude Intervention," *Terapia Psicológica*, 1(1) (2013): 93–100, https://scielo.conicyt.cl/pdf/terpsicol/v31n1/art09.pdf. (The present study compared the effects of a one-week best-possible-self intervention and a one-week gratitude intervention on life satisfaction and optimism. The BPS exercise for three to five minutes led to significant increase in optimism and life satisfaction, above gratitude.)

42   P. M. Loveday, G. P. Lovell, and C. M. Jones, "The Best Possible Selves Intervention: A Review of the Literature to Evaluate Efficacy and Guide Future Research," *Journal of Happiness Studies* 19(2) (2018): 607–628. (Since its inception in 2001, the BPS, activity has been the focus of more than thirty studies, which have shown it to be a viable intervention for increasing optimism, positive affect, health, and well-being. This article critically reviews the findings from the BPS literature and suggests directions for future research.)

43   T. Bipp, A. Kleingeld, H. van Mierlo, and W. Kunde, "The Effect of Subconscious Performance Goals on Academic Performance," *The Journal of Experimental Education* 85(3) (2017): 469–485.

44   "Cogito, ergo sum," *Wikipedia*, last modified November 27, 2019, https://en.wikipedia.org/wiki/Cogito,_ergo_sum.

45   Landy, R. J. (1996). *Persona and performance: The meaning of role in drama, therapy, and everyday life.* Guilford Press.

46   Kok, B. E., Coffey, K. A., Cohn, M. A., Catalino, L. I., Vacharkulksemsuk, T., Algoe, S. B., & Fredrickson, B. L. (2013). How positive emotions build physical health: Perceived positive social

connections account for the upward spiral between positive emotions and vagal tone. *Psychological science, 24*(7), 1123-1132.

47   B. E. Kok, K. A. Coffey, M. A. Cohn, L. I. Catalino, T. Vacharkulksemsuk, S. B. Algoe, M. Brantley, and B. L. Fredrickson, "How Positive Emotions Build Physical Health: Perceived Positive Social Connections Account for the Upward Spiral Between Positive Emotions and Vagal Tone," *Psychological Science* 24(7) (2013): 1123–1132. (The authors hypothesize that an upward-spiral dynamic continually reinforces the tie between positive emotions and physical health, and that this spiral is mediated by people's perceptions of their positive social connections. This experimental evidence identifies one mechanism— perceptions of social connections—through which positive emotions build physical health, indexed as vagal tone.)

48   Ibid.

Chapter 3

49   G. L. Paul, "The Production of Blisters by Hypnotic Suggestion: Another Look," *Psychosomatic Medicine* 25(3) (1963): 233–244.

50   D. G. Hammond, "Integrating Clinical Hypnosis and Neurofeedback," *American Journal of Clinical Hypnosis* 61(4) (2019), 302–321.

51   V. E. Frankl, The Harvard Lectures, 1961, archive reference 19612, (vienna: Viktor Frankl Archives).

52   K. W. Brown and R. M. Ryan, "The Benefits of Being Present: Mindfulness and its Role in Psychological Well-Being," *Journal of Personality and Social Psychology* 84(4) (2003): 822–848. (An experience-sampling study shows that both dispositional and state mindfulness predict self-regulated behavior and positive emotional states. Finally, a clinical intervention study with cancer patients demonstrates that increases in mindfulness over time relate to declines in mood disturbance and stress.)

53   E. R. Tomlinson, O. Yousaf, A. D. Vittersø, and L. Jones, "Dispositional Mindfulness and Psychological Health: A Systematic Review," *Mindfulness* 9(1) (2018): 23–43. (Three main themes emerged, depicting the relationship between DM and psychological health: 1. DM appears to be inversely related to psychopathological symptoms, such as depressive symptoms; 2. DM is positively linked to adaptive cognitive processes, such as less rumination and pain catastrophizing; and 3. DM appears to be associated with better emotional processing and regulation.)

54   M. J. Murphy, L. C. Mermelstein, K. M. Edwards, and C. A. Gidycz, "The Benefits of Dispositional Mindfulness in Physical Health: A Longitudinal Study of Female College Students," *Journal of American College Health* 60(5) (2012): 341–348. (This article examines the relationship between DM, health behaviors—such as sleep, eating, and exercise—and physical health.)

55   M. K. Rasmussen and A. M. Pidgeon, "The Direct and Indirect Benefits of Dispositional Mindfulness on Self-Esteem and Social Anxiety," *Anxiety, Stress, & Coping* 24(2) (2011): 227–233. (The current study investigated relationships between dispositional mindfulness, self-esteem, and social anxiety, using self-report measures.)

56   J. Kabat-Zinn, *Wherever You Go, There You Are: Mindfulness Meditation in Everyday Life* (Hachette Books: 2005): 4.

57   A. Ginsberg, *Cosmopolitan Greetings:* Poems 1986–1992 (New York: HarperCollins, 1995).

58   T. Rashid and M. P. Seligman, *Positive Psychotherapy*: *Clinician Manual* (Oxford University Press, 2018).

Chapter 4

59   Robert M. Sapolsky, *Why Zebras Don't Get Ulcers* (New York: Henry Holt and Co, 2004).

60   B. L. Fredrickson, *Positivity*: *Top-Notch Research Reveals the 3 to 1 Ratio that Will Change Your Life* (New York: Harmony Books, 2009).

61   S. F. Maier and M. E. P. Seligman, "Learned Helplessness at Fifty: Insights from Neuroscience," *Psychological Review* 123(4) (2016): 349–367.

62   M. E. P. Seligman, *Learned Optimism*: *How to Change Your Mind and Your Life* (New York: Vintage Books, 2006).

63   I. D. Yalom and M. Leszcz, *The Theory and Practice of Group Psychotherapy, Fifth Edition* (New York: Basic Books, 2005): 4.

64   C. R. Snyder, A. B. LaPointe, J. Jeffrey Crowson, and S. Early, "Preferences of High- and Low-Hope People for Self-Referential Input," *Cognition & Emotion* 12(6) (1998): 807–823.

65   S. J. Lopez, *Making Hope Happen*: *Create the Future You Want for Yourself and Others* (New York: Simon and Schuster, 2013).

66   K. D. Neff, K. L. Kirkpatrick, and S. S. Rude, "Self-Compassion and Adaptive Psychological Functioning," *Journal of Research in Personality* *41*(1) (2007): 139–154.

67   Yang, Y., Zhang, M., & Kou, Y. (2016). Self-compassion and life satisfaction: The mediating role of hope. *Personality and Individual Differences, 98,* 91-95.

68   L. Shapiro, *Embodied Cognition,* 2nd Edition (New York: Routledge, 2019). (Embodied cognition is a recent development in psychology that practitioners often present as superseding standard cognitive science. Lawrence Shapiro sets out the central themes and debates surrounding embodied cognition, explaining and assessing the work of many of the key figures in the field.)

69   Glenberg, A. M., Havas, D., Becker, R., & Rinck, M. (2005). Grounding language in bodily states. *Grounding cognition: The role of perception and action in memory, language, and thinking,* 115-128.

70   R. Wiseman, *The As If Principle*: *The Radically New Approach to Changing Your Life* (New York: Simon and Schuster, 2014). (The as-if principle offers real, workable solutions for your day-to-day goals while helping you to instantly take control of your emotions.)

71   E. J. Langer, *Counterclockwise: Mindful Health and the Power of Possibility* (New York: Ballantine Books, 2009).

72   M. M. Tugade, and B. L. Fredrickson, "Regulation of Positive Emotions: Emotion Regulation Strategies That Promote Resilience," *Journal of Happiness Studies* 8(3) (2007): 311–333.

73   I. W. Hung and A. A. Labroo, "From Firm Muscles to Firm Willpower: Understanding the Role of Embodied Cognition in Self-Regulation," *Journal of Consumer Research* 37(6) (2011): 1046–1064, https://www.jstor.org/stable/10.1086/657240?seq=1#metadata_info _tab_contents.

74   J. C. Bays, *How to Train a Wild Elephant: And Other Adventures in Mindfulness* (Boulder, CO: Shambhala Publications, 2011).

75   B. Tracy, *Eat that Frog!: 21 Great Ways to Stop Procrastinating and Get More Done in Less Time* (San Francisco: Berrett-Koehler Publishers, 2007).

76   R. Friedman and A. J. Elliot, "The Effect of Arm Crossing on Persistence and Performance," *European Journal of Social Psychology* 38(3) (2008): 449–461.

77   D. R. Carney, A. J. Cuddy, and A. J. Yap, "Power Posing: Brief Nonverbal Displays Affect Neuroendocrine Levels and Risk Tolerance," *Psychological Science* 21(10) (2010): 1363–1368.

78   J. M. Ackerman, C. C. Nocera, and J. A. Bargh, "Incidental Haptic Sensations Influence Social Judgments and Decisions," *Science* 328(5986) (2010): 1712–1715, https://www.ncbi.nlm.nih.gov/pmc/articles/PMC 3005631/.

79   C. B. Zhong and K. Liljenquist, "Washing Away Your Sins: Threatened Morality and Physical Cleansing," *Science* 313(5792) (2006): 1451–1452.

80   K. W. Brown, R. M. Ryan, and J. D. Creswell, "Mindfulness: Theoretical Foundations and Evidence for Its Salutary Effects," *Psychological Inquiry* 18(4) (2007): 211–237.

81   J. Haidt, "The Positive Emotion of Elevation," *Prevention &* *Treatment* 3(1) (March 2000), faculty.virginia.edu/haidtlab/articles/haidt .2000.the-positive-emotion-of-elevation.pub020.pdf.

Chapter 5

82   "Uruguayan Air Force Flight 571," *Wikipedia*, last modified December 2, 2019, https://en.wikipedia.org/wiki/Uruguayan_Air_Force _Flight_571.

83   Gillham, J., Reivich, K., and Seligman, M., [listed as investigators], "Resilience in Children: The Penn Resilience Program for Middle School Students," University of Pennsylvania, Positive Psychology Center, https:// ppc.sas.upenn.edu/research/resilience-children.

84   University of Pennsylvania, Positive Psychology Center, "Resilience Training for the Army," https://ppc.sas.upenn.edu/services/resilience -training-army.

85   C. Peterson and M. E. Seligman, *Character Strengths and Virtues*: *A Handbook and Classification* 1 (Oxford University Press, 2004).

86   American Psychiatric Association, *Diagnostic and Statistical Manual of Mental Disorders* (*DSM-5®*) (Arlington, VA: American Psychiatric Association Publishing, 2013).

87   VIA Institute on Character website, www.viacharacter.org.

88   C. Peterson and M. E. Seligman, *Character Strengths and Virtues*: *A Handbook and Classification* 1 (Oxford University Press, 2004).

89   VIA Institute on Character, "Character Strengths," www.via character.org/character-strengths-via.

90   P. Freidlin, H. Littman-Ovadia, and R. M. Niemiec, "Positive Psychopathology: Social Anxiety Via Character Strengths Underuse and Overuse," *Personality and Individual Differences* 108(2017): 50–54.

91   Ibid.

92   R. Niemiec, "The Overuse of Strengths: 10 Principles," *PsycCRITIQUES* 59(33): (2014), https://psqtest.typepad.com/blogPost PDFs/TheOveruseOfStrengths_8-18-2014.pdf.

93   B. Springsteen, *Born to Run* (New York: Simon and Schuster, 2017).

Chapter 6

94   C. J. Farran, K. A. Herth, and J. M. Popovich, *Hope and Hopelessness*: *Critical Clinical Constructs* (Thousand Oaks, CA: Sage Publications, Inc., 1995).

95   W. Kuyken, F. C. Warren, R. S. Taylor, B. Whalley, C. Crane, G. Bondolfi, et al., "Efficacy of Mindfulness-Based Cognitive Therapy in Prevention of Depressive Relapse: An Individual Patient Data Meta-Analysis from Randomized Trials," *JAMA Psychiatry* 73(6) (2016): 565–574.

96   L. Liu, Z. Gou, and J. Zuo, "Social Support Mediates Loneliness and Depression in Elderly People," *Journal of Health Psychology* 21(5) (2016): 750–758.

97   K. B. Lawlor, "Smart Goals: How the Application of Smart Goals Can Contribute to Achievement of Student Learning Outcomes," in *Developments in Business Simulation and Experiential Learning*: *Proceedings of the Annual ABSEL Conference* 39 (2012), https://absel-ojs-ttu.org/absel /index.php/absel/article/view/90/86.

98   K. Reivich and A. Shatté, *The Resilience Factor*: *7 Essential Skills for Overcoming Life's Inevitable Obstacles* (New York: Broadway Books, 2002).

99   J. M. Grohol, "15 Common Cognitive Distortions," PsychCentral, last updated June 24, 2019, https://psychcentral.com/lib/15-common -cognitive-distortions/.

100   E. Weinstein, "Automatic Negative Thoughts: Got ANTS on the Brain?" last updated May 10, 2019, https://psychcentral.com/blog /automatic-negative-thoughts-got-ants-on-the-brain/.

101   Gillham, J., Reivich, K., and Seligman, M., [listed as investigators], "Resilience in Children: The Penn Resilience Program for Middle School Students," University of Pennsylvania, Positive Psychology Center, https://ppc.sas.upenn.edu/research/resilience-children.

102   Trustees of the University of Pennsylvania, Positive Psychology Center, "Resilience Training for the Army," https://ppc.sas.upenn.edu/services/resilience-training-army.

103   K. McGonigal, "How to make stress your friend," TEDGlobal 2013, https://www.ted.com/talks/kelly_mcgonigal_how_to_make_stress_your_friend.

104   K. McGonigal, *The Upside of Stress: Why Stress Is Good for You, and How to Get Good at It* (New York: Penguin, 2016).

Chapter 7

105   Emily Esfahani Smith, *The Power of Meaning: Crafting a Life that Matters* (New York: Random House, 2017).

106   A. Duckworth, *Grit: The Power of Passion and Perseverance* (New York: Scribner, 2016).

107   C. Schiller, "The As If Principle: Richard Wiseman Shows How Faking It Actually Helps You Make It," *Blinklist Magazine*, December 7, 2014, https://www.blinkist.com/magazine/posts/principle-richard-wiseman-shows-faking-actually-helps-make?utm_source=cpp.

108   K. M. Krpan, E. Kross, M. G. Berman, P. J. Deldin, M. K. Askren, and J. Jonides, "An Everyday Activity as a Treatment for Depression: The Benefits of Expressive Writing for People Diagnosed with Major Depressive Disorder," *Journal of Affective Disorders* 150(3) (2013): 1148–1151.

109   C. E. Ackerman, "83 Benefits of Journaling for Depression, Anxiety, and Stress," November 20, 2019, PositivePsychology.com, https://positivepsychology.com/benefits-of-journaling/.

110   K. M. Robinson, "How Writing in a Journal Helps Manage Depression," WebMD, December 4, 2017, https://www.webmd.com/depression/features/writing-your-way-out-of-depression#1.

111   D. Tomasulo and A. Szucs, "The ACTing Cure: Evidence-Based Group Treatment for People With Intellectual Disabilities," *Dramatherapy*, 37(2–3) (2015): 100–115.

112   D. Tomasulo, *American Snake Pit*: Hope, Grit, and Resilience in *the Wake of Willowbrook* (Fairfax, VA: Stillhouse Press, 2018).

113   D. Tomasulo, "What Is Self-Compassion?" https://www.DanTomasulo.com.

114   Z. Moreno, foreword, in Robert Landry, *The Couch and the Stage*: *Integrating Words and Action in Psychotherapy* (New York: Jason Aronson, 2008), xi.

115   C. Lambert, "The Science of Happiness," *Harvard Magazine*, January–February 2007, https://www.harvardmagazine.com/2007/01/the-science-of-happiness.html.

116   A. Ginsberg, *Cosmopolitan Greetings* (New York: HarperCollins, 1995).

Chapter 8

117   J. Hari, *Lost Connections*: Uncovering the Real Causes of Depression— *And the Unexpected Solutions* (Bloomsbury Publishing plc, 2019).

118   L. Mineo, "Good Genes Are Nice, But Joy Is Better," *The Harvard Gazette*, April 11, 2017, https://news.harvard.edu/gazette/story/2017/04/over-nearly-80-years-harvard-study-has-been-showing-how-to-live-a-healthy-and-happy-life/.

119   R. Waldinger, "What Makes a Good Life? Lessons from the Longest Study on Happiness," TEDxBeaconStreet, November 2015, https://www.ted.com/talks/robert_waldinger_what_makes_a_good_life_lessons_from_the_longest_study_on_happiness?language=en.

120   S. Stossel, "What Makes Us Happy, Revisited," *The Atlantic*, May 2013, https://www.theatlantic.com/magazine/archive/2013/05/thanks-mom/309287/.

121   D. J. Tomasulo, "The Virtual Gratitude Visit (VGV): Using Psychodrama and Role-Playing as a Positive Intervention," in *Positive Psychological Intervention Design and Protocols for Multi-Cultural Contexts* (New York: Springer, 2019): 405–413.

122   M. E. Seligman, T. A. Steen, N. Park, and C. Peterson, "Positive Psychology Progress: Empirical Validation of Interventions," *American Psychologist* 60(5) (2005): 410.

123   J. W. Koo, "Brain-Derived Neurotrophic Factor Is a Miracle Fertilizer for Our Brain?" *Atlas of Science*, June 22, 2016, https://atlasofscience.org/brain-derived-neurotrophic-factor-is-a-miracle-fertilizer-for-our-brain/.

124   S. Douglas, "Running from the Pain," *Slate*, March 12, 2018, https://slate.com/technology/2018/03/exercise-is-as-effective-as-antidepressants-for-many-cases-of-depression.html.

125   E. Jaffe, "The Psychological Study of Smiling," *APS Observer* 23(10) (2011), https://www.psychologicalscience.org/observer/the-psychological-study-of-smiling.

126   B. Fredrickson, *Love 2.0*: *How Our Supreme Emotion Affects Everything We Feel, Think, Do, and Become* (New York: Avery, 2013); "The Big Idea: Barbara Fredrickson on Love 2.0." *The Daily Beast*, July 12, 2017, https://www.thedailybeast.com/the-big-idea-barbara-fredrickson-on-love20.

127   S. Carnazzi, "Kintsugi: the Art of Precious Scars," *Lifegate*, date unknown, https://www.lifegate.com/people/lifestyle/kintsugi.

128   S. L. Gable, H. T. Reis, E. A. Impett, and E. R. Asher, "What Do You Do When Things Go Right?: The Intrapersonal and Interpersonal Benefits of Sharing Positive Events," *Journal of Personality and Social Psychology* 87(2) (2004): 228–245.

129   E. E. Smith, "Masters of Love," *The Atlantic*, June 12, 2014, https://www.theatlantic.com/health/archive/2014/06/happily-ever-after/372573/.

Chapter 9

130   "The Power of the Placebo Effect," Harvard Health Publishing, May 2017, last updated August 9, 2019, https://www.health.harvard.edu/mental-health/the-power-of-the-placebo-effect.

131   M. Talbot, "The Placebo Prescription," *The New York Times Magazine*, January 9, 2000, https://www.nytimes.com/2000/01/09/magazine/the-placebo-prescription.html.

132   T. Rashid and M. P. Seligman, *Positive Psychotherapy: Clinician Manual* (Oxford University Press, 2018).

133   J. Dispenza, *You Are the Placebo: Making Your Mind Matter* (Carlsbad, CA: Hay House, Inc., 2014).

134   P. Enck and W. Häuser, "Beware the Nocebo Effect," *The New York Times*, August 10, 2012, https://www.nytimes.com/2012/08/12/opinion/sunday/beware-the-nocebo-effect.html.

135   L. Colloca and F. G. Miller, "The Nocebo Effect and Its Relevance for Clinical Practice," *Psychosomatic Medicine* 73(7) (2011): 598–603.

136   A. Ginsberg, *Spontaneous Mind: Selected Interviews, 1958–1996* (New York: Harper Collins, 2002), 15.

137   J. Clear, *Atomic Habits: An Easy and Proven Way to Build Good Habits and Break Bad Ones* (New York: Avery, 2018), 28.

138   B. H. Lipton, *The Biology of Belief 10th Anniversary Edition: Unleashing the Power of Consciousness, Matter & Miracles* (Carlsbad, CA: Hay House, 2015).

Dan Tomasulo, PhD, is core faculty at the Spirituality Mind Body Institute (SMBI) at Teachers College, Columbia University; and honored by *Sharecare* as one of the top ten online influencers on the issue of depression. He holds a PhD in psychology, MFA in writing, and a master of applied positive psychology from the University of Pennsylvania. A highly sought-after international speaker on topics relating to applied positive psychology, he authors the daily column, Ask the Therapist, and the *Learned Hopefulness* blog for www.psych central.com. His award-winning memoir, *American Snake Pit*, was released in 2018.

Foreword writer **Scott Barry Kaufman, PhD**, is host of *The Psychology Podcast*, and author of *Transcend*.

Real change *is* possible

For more than forty-five years, New Harbinger has published proven-effective self-help books and pioneering workbooks to help readers of all ages and backgrounds improve mental health and well-being, and achieve lasting personal growth. In addition, our spirituality books offer profound guidance for deepening awareness and cultivating healing, self-discovery, and fulfillment.

Founded by psychologist Matthew McKay and Patrick Fanning, New Harbinger is proud to be an independent, employee-owned company. Our books reflect our core values of integrity, innovation, commitment, sustainability, compassion, and trust. Written by leaders in the field and recommended by therapists worldwide, New Harbinger books are practical, accessible, and provide real tools for real change.

newharbingerpublications

MORE BOOKS *from*
NEW HARBINGER PUBLICATIONS

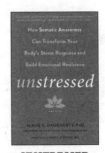